Top 10 Tips For Your Top 10 Customers

A Key Account Management Handbook

The **SYSTEMS**

The **STRATEGIES**

The **SKILLS**

By David Ventura & Phil Jesson

© 2019 KAMguru

Published by New Generation Publishing in 2019

Copyright © David Ventura & Phil Jesson 2019

First Edition

The author asserts the moral right under the Copyright, Designs and Patents Act 1988 to be identified as the author of this work.

All Rights reserved. No part of this publication may be reproduced, stored in a retrieval system or transmitted, in any form or by any means without the prior consent of the author, nor be otherwise circulated in any form of binding or cover other than that which it is published and without a similar condition being imposed on the subsequent purchaser.

ISBN: 978-1-78955-438-0

www.newgeneration-publishing.com

CONTENTS

Acknowledgements iv
About the Authors vi
Introduction: 1
Tip one: Establish KAM clarity and focus 8
Tip two: Work as a Partner, not a supplier 13
Tip three: Add value, not cost 29
Tip four: Build your business from the "outside-in" 36
Tip five: Create the XX Factor 47
Tip six: Become an expert in their world 59
Tip seven: Find the right round pegs 65
Tip eight: Lead KAM as a team sport 71
Tip nine: Build KAMPlans 82
Tip ten: Work as a KAMeleon 106
Appendix .... Where To Next? 121

Acknowledgements

We would like to thank our clients for their fantastic support over many happy years.

Half this book would be taken up if we were to mention everyone by name, so perhaps we could offer a collective very big "thank-you" to the key decision makers (and their many conference and training participants) from our key accounts including:-

FedEx	Tarmac	Interflora
Grant Thornton	Marsh	Remploy
Pirelli	Michelin	EDF Energy
Honeywell	Pertemps	GRS Roadstone
Network Rail	CIMA	Exel Logistics
Bass Brewers	Henley Mgt College	Home Serve
Tunstall Healthcare	Yusen Logistics	Premier Percussion

There are many KAM (Key Account Management) strategies, systems and skills featured in the book but clearly we do not have the copyright on the right answer. During the course of our work, we have always considered ourselves to be "work in progress" and have enjoyed being co-learners with our clients.

A big thank-you, then, to the successful and inspirational senior executives who have been our "partners" on the journey (and also an absolute joy to work with!) They include Alan Buckle, Dave Sharratt, Christine Adames, Peter Lane, Jim Dickens, Tracey Bovingdon, Jon Fisher, Paul Willmott, Martin Hill, Jon Lowe, Steve Richardson, Elizabeth Mills,

Mark Bent, Nick Drew and Alan Ratcliffe. They have all led their respective "KAMpaigns" to new heights.

In particular, our relationship with the CEO peer-group networking world during the last decade has been particularly enjoyable, satisfying and productive so we would like to thank the leaders, chairs and members in that sector including Vistage, The Academy for Chief Executives, MD2MD, The Executive Foundation and Elite Recruitment Network.

Our loyal band of colleagues, associates and supporters also deserve a special mention. In particular, Joanna Jesson, Martin Dunkerley, Ken Minor, Richard Ellison Smith, Ken Allison, Tony Bray, Ray Gudge, Simon Kelly, Graham Jones, Simon Hazeldine and Fred Robson.

Thank you for putting your head, heart and soul into creating some outstanding results. Your competence, confidence and commitment has created sustainable, profitable change for many clients who, as a result, now stand out from their competitors, rather than stand up to them!

About the Authors

DAVID VENTURA

David is a thought-provoking speaker who helps Senior Leaders and their teams improve profitability and performance, bringing to life the principles of increasing results by improving relationships with an organisation's most important customers.

David has spent over 12 years in a variety of commercial and leadership roles across numerous sectors, including Retail, IT and Telecoms, with a proven track record in generating new business and growth from the existing customer base.

Having started his career in the entertainment industry, David now works as a speaker, corporate trainer and coach, dedicating his time to helping organisations grow revenues, empower employees and reach full potential by delivering highly engaging and 'output focused' workshops. His passion for 'performance' has carried through some core principles of Customer Growth;

- The key to any great 'performance' is integrity and authenticity. The same applies to business.
- If 'people buy from people' then rapport and relationship skills are the most powerful skills to master in business.
- Sales can often be seen as a downstream result of Service Excellence.

PHIL JESSON

Phil Jesson started his career as an Army Officer and then moved into the sales and marketing world, or "planet customer" as he prefers to call it. He worked with a number of international companies before setting up his own training and consulting business.

As a consultant, coach, professional speaker and author he has worked with many high-profile clients but has also enjoyed the SME community where he is well-known within the CEO peer-group networking world.

He wrote the highly-acclaimed business novel "Piranhas In The Bidet" and is also a co-founder of www.saleschatshow.com - the online audio sales resource that helps sales leaders and their people drive sales forward.

Phil lives in Leicestershire with his wife Joanna and enjoys music, gardening, being a presenter on hospital radio and charity work. He supports Aston Villa on Saturdays ....and often has to "seek counselling on Mondays!"

Introduction:

The Italian economist and philosopher, Vilfredo Pareto, concluded in 1896 that "there is an imbalance between causes and results, inputs and outputs and effect and reward."

In one of his studies he established that "80% of Italy's wealth is in the hands of 20% of its people." There is some remarkable consistency here and interestingly, in a 1989 study, researchers found that 82.7% of the world's GDP was in the hands of 20% of its people.

The pareto principle also has an interesting formula!	$\log N = \log A + m \log x$

OK. So, we lied about the word "interesting", but it is important, as you will see. Pareto did not name the 80-20 rule after himself. In the 1930s, quality guru Joseph Juran named the rule as the "Pareto Principle" and it has been with us ever since.

Have a look around - it is everywhere..

At home:

- 80% of the time we wear 20% of our clothes
- 80% of the time we walk on 20% of our carpets
- 80% of our phone calls are to 20% of people in our network (although if you have a teenage daughter all recognised theories on telephone behaviour should be abandoned!)

In society:

- 80% of accidents are caused by 20% of drivers
- 80% of famine is confined to 20% of countries
- 80% of disruption in schools is caused by 20% of pupils

At work:

- 80% of factory quality problems are caused by 20% of the workforce
- 80% of any market is in the hands of 20% of the suppliers in that market
- 80% of absenteeism is caused by 20% of the workforce

If Vilfredo was alive today, he would see that the 80-20 principle is still alive and well. He would see us listening to 20% of our music for 80% of the time. He would look at the world of professional and competitive sport and see that 20% of an athlete's training regime has 80% of the impact. If he walked into the business world today, he would see that the Pareto Principle is recognised, implemented and being managed on a daily basis.

- IT managers know that 20% of computer code contains 80% of the errors.
- Health and Safety managers know that 20% of hazards account for 80% of injuries
- Sales and Marketing managers and directors in the B2B world know that 20% of their customers (the key accounts) often produce 80% of the business.

In many ways, the 80-20 law has now become the first rule of business – look after your most important customers before someone else does!

So, as you flick through the early pages of this key account management handbook, we need to build a strong case around relevance and why the book is "right for its time".

Things are changing out there in the marketplace.

1. Firstly, the "more business from fewer customers" trend is continuing and is showing no sign of slowing up. In one recent study, researchers found that 4% of an organisation's customers often produce around 64% of the business. That's huge!

2. The customer base is changing. Those at the smaller end are now managed on a transactional model (often via technology and telephone), the middle-ground has disappeared (along with the legions of field-based sales executives that used to manage them) and key accounts at the top-end are now looking for a consultative partnership that will add value and help them transform their businesses. We look at that in chapters two and three.

3. The traditional gaps that used to exist between products, packaging, pricing and distribution etc have narrowed and can be easily copied by competitors. Today, in the eyes of the customer, "everyone is selling the same sort of thing." However, the one thing that cannot be copied is your people and the way that they build relationships and interact with your customers.

   For many companies today, relationship management is their _only_ differentiator. It has become the home of competitive advantage. It is the strategy that helps organisations stand out from their competitors rather than stand up to them.

4. There is one major problem with sales training programmes - they work! They train people how to sell - but they don't train people to understand why the other person is likely to buy.

    The old ABC ("always be closing") has been replaced by the new ABC (analyse how the customer thinks and works, build a bridge to their world and communicate in their language not yours).

    This is something that we look at in chapter ten. In today's world, all key account teams need to understand buyer psychology, motivation and behaviour …….it is the key to success.

5. But some things never change, like human nature. Sometimes, the once sharp and skilful management of an important customer relationship can slip into a comfortable routine and habit, which then becomes a complacent rut, before deepening into a cavern of arrogance. Research shows that 9% of customers switch suppliers due to price-related issues but 68% switch because of "perceived indifference"……..customers think we don't care anymore!

    These surveys also show that customer loyalty has changed over the last ten years and that just meeting customer expectations is not enough. Expectations have to be exceeded at every stage of the customer's journey and that's something we look at in chapter five.

    We believe that it is impossible to make improvements unless you know where you are starting from and we hope that you will use the book as a "health check" on how you and your colleagues are currently performing in all matters key account management. You will then be able to use the book's tactics, tools and techniques to improve the situation.

The book will help you establish where you are starting from in three key areas:-

- How well KAM strategies are working
- How well KAM systems are working
- How well KAM skills are working.

We think that the book will REMIND you of things you have seen and done before (but maybe forgotten), REASSURE you that what you are currently doing, in many areas, is "right" and will REVEAL some new ideas and thinking suited to the world of the future.

Think of KAM strategies, systems and skills as the legs of a three-legged stool. You can't get a three-legged stool to stand up on either one or two of its legs - all three legs have to be working effectively for it to stand up. We believe that the book will help you develop all three "legs" and help you and your organisation become a leader in its field.

And whilst we are on the subject of being a leader, let's have a look at what that actually means. It is not just about implementing best practice - by definition someone in your sector, or a different sector, is already up and running with those strategies, systems or skills. Best practice, by definition, already exists. Being a leader is about identifying and implementing "next practice" not best practice.

Remember Dick Fosbury? He was the American high jumper who won the gold medal at the Olympic Games in Mexico City in 1968. He knew that he was never going to win the gold medal by implementing best practice (going over the bar forwards, the same as everyone else). He developed the "Fosbury Flop" and was the first to go over the bar backwards. He identified and implemented next practice which produced a spectacular result.

So, you may want to use this book to identify how you are going to "do a Fosbury" and go over the key account management bar backwards and, in the process, stand out from your competitors not stand up to them, as we said earlier.

Finally, a few words about "implementation". The journey from bright idea to profitable, sustainable reality is rarely straightforward. So there are plenty of tools and helpful advice available on our www.kamguru.com, www.saleschatshow.com and www.strategicbridges.co.uk websites.

We urge you to take action and make excellence in key account management a daily habit. Deciding to do something is not the same as actually doing something. Please remember that perfectionism is an illness not a quality - good plans actioned today are usually better than perfect plans actioned next month. When you make KAM a daily habit you will find that everyone benefits:-

- ✓ You will exceed customer expectations, not just meet them
- ✓ Key account loyalty and retention will improve
- ✓ Profitability improves – theirs and yours
- ✓ You will be able to grow your business through low-cost referrals

- ✓ You will have a better understanding of your customer's world
- ✓ You will develop an image of being a leading-edge, customer-focused business
- ✓ Staff retention and recruitment will improve
- ✓ You will feel more in alignment with your customers' timings and business cycles
- ✓ You will develop a long-term strategic conversation with the customer
- ✓ Your organisation will be seen as the industry expert
- ✓ You will be able to charge more for the great value that you are creating
- ✓ Directors will spend less time on admin and more time leading at the sharp end
- ✓ Happy customers will give you testimonials
- ✓ Culturally, account management will be seen as a team sport across your business
- ✓ Customers will enjoy a collaborative and constructive partnership with you
- ✓ You will be adding value in the customer's boardroom
- ✓ Your organisation will be perceived as a trusted partner
- ✓ Your account managers will enjoy more satisfaction and less frustration
- ✓ Account managers and support staff will work as an effective team
- ✓ You will stand out from competitors not just stand up to them

Good luck ....and enjoy the journey!

David and Phil

Tip one: Establish KAM clarity and focus

The opening chapter of the book is the shortest as it is pure common sense. But, there again, common sense is not necessarily common practice so maybe we shouldn't be apologising for it.

Think of your business in the future, the sales targets and objectives that you and your people have, and the plans to achieve them. Fortunately, business development is not rocket science and, within your business pipeline, there are only four places where sales can actually come from:-

SUSPECTS	PROSPECTS	CUSTOMERS	KEY ACCOUNTS
Companies who don't know you and you don't know them	Contacted but not yet buying from you	People buying from you on a regular basis	?

So, let's have a look at that right-hand box and how you define exactly what a key account is. Who are those people and what makes them "key?" There is no right answer here and, to date, we have come across many different ways that our clients have defined it:-

- Are they your largest customers, by volume, looking back in time?

- But should history come into it? Some of our readers will consider a "key account" to be major customers or major prospects with the greatest potential value?

- Or are key accounts those that are coming up for major contract re-negotiation?

- Or major customers that have had some major issues with your products and service and are now in "intensive care"?

- Perhaps key accounts are those where you are making an "unacceptable profit" and you need to deliver an exceptional level of service to justify it?

- Key accounts might also be important lost customers you want to win back

- Or a dream prospect that you would like in the future – the sort of organisation that would change the fortunes of your business if you had them on board?

- They could be a competitor's major customers that are vulnerable for a period of time. For example, if a competitor's key account manager has recently moved on, their vacant territory might present a window of opportunity for a short period of time.

- Whilst we are on the subject of competitors, a key account might be one of your major customers that is being targeted and courted by your competitors. Do you know who these accounts are?

- Key accounts could also be a customer where, if you lost them, your business would feel the repercussions immediately with major consequences like redundancies or cut-backs.

- If you have a multi-site customer operation with dozens of people across the country, you might simply ask your managers to work on three key accounts that are vital to their branch......................and then allow the team to tell you what their criteria are for a key account!

- But hang on a minute, let's allow the Finance Directors to have a say. For them, perhaps key accounts are the 20% of customers generating 80% of the profits? They would say that profit is the thing that matters!

- And what about those small accounts that spend next to nothing but have huge prestige value – the sort of door-opener names that when you mention them in the marketplace, prospects say "Wow, you are working with them, well you had better come and talk to us then!"

- One of our clients decided that a key account needed to have "Five Essentials" and "Five Desirables"

Five Essentials	Five Desirables
<ul><li>"Headroom" i.e. potential for growth</li><li>Good existing relationships</li><li>Same values and beliefs</li><li>Where quality is more important than price</li><li>Account is in target growth market</li></ul>	<ul><li>Customer unaffected by outside factors</li><li>They have prestige value</li><li>Scope for broadening services</li><li>Competitor experiencing problems</li><li>Their business is growing</li></ul>

Clearly there is no "single right answer" as far as the definition of a key account is concerned but it's important that you have a right answer that fits your business, and that your people know and understand who the key accounts are.

Our work often starts in the boardroom where there is a "7 out of 10" level of understanding on this issue, but when we leave the boardroom and start to talk to, and work with, teams of people we are often horrified to find that there is a 3 out of 10 level of understanding. Directors and their people may only be physically ten metres apart, but they are often miles adrift on KAM clarity and focus.

To summarise, you may want to discuss some of these questions with your colleagues.

HEALTH CHECK QUESTIONS

1. What is the definition of a key account within your business?
2. So, who are they?
3. Do your people know who they are and why they are "key"?
4. How profitable are they today - do some key accounts need "managing out?"
5. When your sales people go hunting for new customers do you ask them to look for "quality key accounts" with clear selection criteria or will any old customer do?!

CONCLUSIONS

- Ideally, and strategically, you should be working with the customers that you really want to work with, and your competitors should be working with the rest!

- Key accounts are not "customers with a few more oooooooos on the end of them." They are different and the difference needs to be clarified and managed.

- The ideal organisation, and the one with the best chances of success, is one where if you asked anyone from the chairman down to the newest recruit who the key accounts are you would get the same answer

- Strive for next practice not best practice!

Tip two: Work as a Partner, not a supplier

Time for a four-square matrix! As you know, all management consultants, authors and professional speakers have to refer to a four-square matrix from time to time otherwise we wither and die. It's as simple as that!

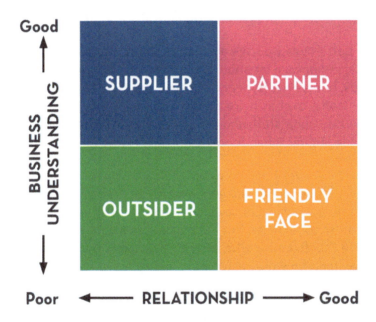

Let's give you a quick conducted tour around the matrix:-

Bottom Left – here we have a situation where your account manager has a poor ability to develop relationships and a poor ability to understand the customer's business. He or she is likely to be perceived as an OUTSIDER and their approach would probably result in the customer questioning their interest and competence thinking "which planet are you on??"

Bottom Right – this is the quadrant frequented by a large number of account managers. In this box, they tend to be brilliant at the relationship building stuff but poor at really understanding the customer's business. They are perceived as a FRIENDLY FACE. But they do the relationship building stuff really well and know favourite football teams, remember important details about the customer's family and make the right noises, often over a second cup of coffee. However, their chat often goes on far too long and by the time they are ready to start the call...........the customer is looking at a watch, signalling that it is the end of the call.

Top Left – here we have a situation where the account manager knows a lot about the customer's business and its needs, but s/he is not good at relationship building. They often come over as being a little wooden or mechanical, but they know their stuff, and are sometimes perceived as a walking technical handbook.

If you have ever been on a joint visit with one of these SUPPLIER account managers, you will probably have seen them do something, or say something, that has left the customer speechless. But the account manager doesn't realise this, because s/he lacks the "sensors" that let them understand how the customer is feeling.

Top Right – this is the ideal situation i.e. one where the account manager has excellent relationship building skills and an excellent understanding of the customer's business. Account managers who are PARTNERS see themselves as equals, are collaborative team players, take control in a friendly, confident and assertive manner, are high on questions and listening and low on talking.

They seek win-win outcomes, work with medium to long-term outcomes, are seen as trusted advisors and come to the table with new ideas. They lead, challenge and encourage and are comfortable with the occasional bit of creative tension if it generates new thinking.

"A gossip is one who talks to you about others. A bore is someone who talks to you about himself. A brilliant conversationalist is one who talks to you about yourself!"

~ Lisa Kirk ~

Time for two stories. Firstly, let's give you an example of an account manager working in total alignment with the horizontal axis........i.e. getting the "relationship stuff" right.

This is the story of account manager Tim, who needed to meet up with Bill, an important industry name and a new board-level decision maker at an existing customer that Tim had worked with for three years. It was a customer that Tim was keen to retain in view of its size and potential.

Whilst sitting in another customer's reception area one day, Tim was browsing through a trade magazine and came across an article on Bill. It was one of those light-hearted "inside the back cover" features where the journalist asked Bill a number of questions about his life and interests, including "Where is your favourite holiday destination?" "What music do you like?" and "If you won the Lottery what would you buy?"

Tim noticed Bill's answers to two questions in particular............

Journalist: What would your perfect meal be?

Bill: Definitely something Greek, but I don't need to smash the plate!

Journalist: If you could put the clocks back, which career would you pursue?

Bill: That's an interesting one! I would go to University and then become an architect.

When Tim phoned Bill in Liverpool to introduce himself and book an appointment, he deliberately invited Bill down to Birmingham for a meeting that would start at 1200. Now put yourself in Bill's position - the timing and location of the meeting suggests that there might be a spot of lunch on offer and, in view of the return journey time, he might as well allocate the whole day.

The meeting went well and Tim introduced Bill to his delivery and support colleagues and, together, they explored the things that were important to Bill in terms of their ongoing relationship.

Lunchtime arrived. Guess where they took Bill? Yes, to a Greek restaurant - his favourite type of food. But it wasn't "any Greek restaurant", it was a converted Church on the outskirts of Birmingham and apparently Bill spent much of the lunch hour gazing up at the amazing architecture and conversion work.

There was no mention of the article in the trade magazine, but Bill would have been impressed, no doubt, with the genuine attempt by Tim and his colleagues to work with him in a tailored way. It is a great example of influencing with integrity.

Let's give you an example of the vertical axis running up the left-hand side of the matrix...........a great story that illustrates the level of knowledge needed to really understand the key account's business.

Imagine that one of your account managers is going to visit their most important key account. Picture your account manager and the building they are entering. They meet their usual friendly contact who invites them down the corridor to the meeting room where there is plenty of tea, coffee and biscuits available.

Customer: Thanks for coming in to see us today. Bearing in mind our future needs, there are quite a few things I want to talk about.

Your account manager: Great, I've been looking forward to seeing you again.

Customer: But when I spoke to you on the phone the other day, I forgot to tell you that there would be four of us in the meeting today. You, me and two new managers who have recently joined my team – they will have a day-to-day involvement with you and your company, so I have asked them to sit in today. They will be joining us in ten minutes.

Your account manager: Fine. I am looking forward to meeting them.

Customer: So...........in view of the two new faces today I thought it would be a good thing to start the meeting with a short presentation from you.

Your account manager (reaching for their laptop): Sure, I can do that. No problem.

Customer: Ah..............but when I say "a short presentation from you" I don't mean a power-point presentation on your organisation. As we have worked with you for the last three years and see you very much as a partner and dotted-line member of our team, I would like you to deliver a short presentation on your understanding of our business.

Your account manager (looking a little flustered):
Oh........errr......right.

Customer: So, include in your presentation all the usual stuff..........your understanding of our short-term, medium-term and long-term objectives. Put in your understanding of some of the things going on in our marketplace. You must know all about our competitors – who is on the way up and who is on the way out – you may want to include that. We had a board meeting yesterday – you know the sort of things that we talk about. I'm sure you must look at our website from time to time, so you may want to include our chairman's recent comments on the home page and how your company can help us achieve his goals and aspirations.

Your account manager (now looking very flustered):
Yes..............errr................could I just pop out for a minute. Where is the toilet?

I think we should leave that story there, but it does illustrate some key points.

Key account management is not new and it is not difficult. It is, in many ways, a "business basic".......and that is that if you are an expert in the customer's world you never have to sell again. Doors just keep opening. You are rewarded for your understanding of the customer's business and the great value you are adding. You become experts in their stuff and stop talking about your stuff!

> We once worked with a labelling/printing business led by a CEO called Alistair. Upon arrival, he was determined to change the company culture and make it more customer-focused.
>
> Within days he put in place two key strategies:
>
> He asked the meaning of life question i.e. "What business are we in?" Not surprisingly, the answer he received was "That's obvious boss, we are in the printing business".
>
> Alistair pointed out that as 82% of their business came from the vegetable, meat and dairy markets they were not in the printing business at all……….they were in the food business!
>
> He explained that he would be removing magazines like "British Printer" and "Printing Monthly" from the reception area and the canteen and replacing them with magazines like "Food and Drink" and "Food Producers Digest"…….the sorts of magazines that their customers were reading.
>
> He restructured the production floor. Instead of dozens of people and machines trying to be all things to all customers, he created three production lines, each dedicated to a key market.
>
> The lads and lasses on the production floor were soon known as the "veggies", the "beefies" or the "milkies". Within a matter of months, Alistair started to see a return on his strategies. The whole business was now aligned with the issues, needs and expectations of its customers. When key customers came to visit the factory, they were often amazed and impressed by the knowledge of Alistair's people ………who were now experts in the customer's world.

So, we are clearly banging and promoting the "partnership" drum here but how would you know that you are a partner rather than a supplier? What would the "partnership indicators" be? What would you see, feel or hear that would confirm that you are going in the right direction?

Here are some examples of Partnership Indicators:-

1. The key account tells you that you are a partner because you have asked the question "do you see us as a partner or a supplier?"

2. There is clear evidence of added value and ROI i.e. the numbers make sense – we have either helped the customer to reduce costs or increase sales – or both!

3. You understand their future strategy because you are genuinely interested in understanding where they are today, where they are going in the future and how they are going to get there (and where you can help along that journey of course)

4. They give you confidential information, often starting with the words "I shouldn't really be telling you this but.........." or "keep this under your hat as 95% of our people don't know what I am about to tell you.........." This indicator is a great example of trust which, as we all know, is a vital ingredient in any successful and sustainable relationship.

5. There are no nasty surprises in the relationship. Will there be challenges? Yes. Will there be problems? Probably yes. But if things are working well, your friends and allies in the account will tip you off, so there will be no nasty surprises.

6. Strong multi-level relationships. Key account management is a team sport so the indicator here is that probably 2-4 people from your company are in contact with 2-4 people from the key account.

   They should be at different levels – some should be decision makers and some should be decision influencers. Some conversations would be "strategic" and some would be "day-to-day".

By the way, if your account manager leaves your company and takes the key account customer with them, then clearly this multi-level contact strategy won't have been happening. Your organisation should own the key account, not the account manager.

7. More sales and profit as time goes by i.e. you are selling more of the same or the customer is now buying additional products and services from you.

8. They accept your new products and services. They do this willingly – they don't put you through hoops of fire, as they may have done when you first came on board. Maybe they say something like "OK, if you are saying that we would get some value from this new product of yours we will give it a go - we trust your judgement so let's see how it performs during the next six months."

9. Price resistance drops, over time. This issue may never disappear completely but ideally 'price' should be less of an issue than it once was, in view of the value they have been experiencing.

10. They ask for advice, not just on your core offering. They value your thoughts and input as they now see you as a consultant to their business. Often it is as simple as the customer saying something like "We are thinking of changing our structure to improve productivity..........any thoughts or advice?"

11. You have a rolling agreement, not a fixed-term contract. You might view a fixed-term contract as being more favourable than ad-hoc business, but fixed-term contracts are what suppliers are offered. Partners are treated differently. They often enjoy a rolling contract.

Imagine a three-year contract has been secured and that twelve months have elapsed. If the customer is completely satisfied with your company and its performance, you might be able to roll the contract back up to three years.

Rolling contracts are also a great irritant and deterrent to your competitors. Every time they check their diaries and think of approaching your key account, they don't get past Reception as they are told "Sorry, we have a three-year contract with another company............and we are delighted with the service we receive."

12. Reverse hospitality i.e. they pay! Many companies "buy business" with lavish corporate hospitality but this indicator is quite different. This is the customer treating <u>you</u> and taking you and your partner to the tennis..........or the concert.......or the nice restaurant.

13. They invite you to shape the tender – this is a great opportunity for you to add value and, probably, a blind eye will be turned when you include your unique products or processes in the tender.

14. Joint action plans are in place. At the end of a routine call, the customer has probably made some notes, likewise your account manager. But this is your account manager going up a gear and proactively managing the relationship (and saving them time and effort in the process). Maybe it would sound something like "Thanks, Chris, I've really enjoyed the meeting today. I will get the joint action plan drawn up and emailed back to you later today. It will cover the four action points I'm going to look at and the couple of points you said you would look into."

At the next meeting, you might find someone attending who missed the first meeting.

They are going to love you when you say "Nice to meet you. Here is a hard copy of the action plan following my meeting with Chris a couple of weeks ago."

15. They give you referrals. This is the sound of more "trust doors" being opened for your organisation. If a customer gives you a referral, they must feel happy before considering introducing you to another team/division/sister company. Digital marketing experts tell us that in the future customers will source the companies they want to work with in one of two ways – they will either "Google it" or be guided by personal recommendations ....which is exactly what a referral is.

16. Case studies and testimonials. The happy customer agrees to feature in a piece of your marketing and is happy to "tell the story" and the benefits of working with you etc.

17. Two logos appear side by side – maybe on the customer's website and marketing materials – or yours

18. Tolerance in the event of a problem i.e. they do not "lose it" and become angry and animated. They might say "OK, we are not happy, as you know, but we know that you will be working around the clock to resolve this. Let us know how we can help."

19. Feedback is welcomed and dealt with openly. One of the great indicators of a mature, adult, effective partnership is that both sides can talk openly and honestly, without anyone "taking their bat home." Everyone signs up to the belief that there is no such thing as bad feedback and that any feedback is a source of learning and continuous improvement.

20. They bend the rules to accommodate you. An example of this might be something like the duration of the contract. Although the terms of a contract may suggest that it is up for renewal on an annual basis the customer might say something like "I've been thinking............bearing in mind the tremendous amount of work that you and your colleagues have put into this, we are going to let the contract run for another year without putting it out to tender."

Not surprisingly, we have come across many more Partnership Indicators:-

21. You are their first point of contact.
22. Changes in personnel (yours or theirs) do not affect the relationship.
23. You are involved in creating their goals and strategies
24. Relationships develop into genuine friendships outside work.
25. You are copied-in on their emails.
26. You help to train their staff.
27. Your phone call and meeting requests are always granted.
28. Alignment of plans and timings ......i.e. if they have a July-June business year and you have a Jan-December business year then your plans and timings are built around their business year, not yours.
29. You share the costs and rewards.
30. They see you as a dotted-line member of their team
31. They agree to your ongoing and regular price increases
32. They attend your meetings and conferences to provide feedback.
33. They willingly get involved in your customer research
34. Your customer contacts fight your corner in front of their colleagues
35. They regard you as the industry expert.
36. There is a culture fit between your two organisations
37. They offer you exclusivity.
38. You have an office or workspace on their premises.
39. They join your social media networking groups
40. They commit, in writing, to a long-term relationship

Back to the first 20 Partnership Indicators - here they are, being used as a checklist. You will notice that the key account in question scores 13 out of 20 today. If, in three months' time, the score rises to 15 or 16 out of 20 then that would be simple, measurable, one page or one screen progress that can be shared across your organisation.

No.	Partnership Indicators	✓ ✗
1	They tell you that you are a partner	✓
2	There is clear evidence of added value and ROI	✓
3	You understand their future strategy	✗
4	They give you confidential information	✓
5	There are no nasty surprises in the relationship	✓
6	Strong multi-level relationships	✗
7	More sales and profit	✓
8	They accept your suggestion for new products	✓
9	Price resistance drops, over time	✗
10	They ask for advice - not just on your core services	✓
11	You have a rolling agreement, not fixed term	✗
12	Reverse hospitality - they pay!	✓
13	They invite you to shape tenders etc	✓
14	Joint action plans in place	✗
15	They give you referrals	✓
16	Case studies and testimonials	✓
17	Logos appear side by side	✓
18	Tolerance in the event of a problem	✓
19	All feedback is welcomed and dealt with openly	✗
20	They bend the rules to accommodate you	✗
Totals		13/20

Back to CEO Alistair (remember him and the two strategies for his printing/food business?)

Here is his third strategy:-

Alistair didn't have a "top ten" population of key accounts - he had a top five. So, every three months, at the company's quarterly team briefing in the canteen, he created a great KPI by adding together the Partnership Indicator scores for his top five key accounts. He would say something like this:-

"Just so you know, the partnership indicator score for our top five customers has risen from 58 out of 100 to 71 out of 100. Well done everyone - that is a great result and I am now going to hand over to Brian who will explain how we have managed to achieve this and what we are planning to do to get the score up to 80 by Christmas"

But the twenty partnership indicators featured on the checklist example may not be right for your company. The important thing is to build a list of partnership indicators that are right for you.

A couple of years ago we worked with a major logistics company in Northampton and the Account Directors argued that some of the Partnership Indicators needed to be tailored to each of their vertical markets. The CEO, Sarah, listened to their feedback and gave a very simple and effective response. Here is her email on the subject............

Good morning one and all. I enjoyed the meeting and would like to thank you for your thoughts and feedback. This is what we are going to do:-

I need to compare like with like, so we will all have 20 partnership indicators - I don't want an "apples and pears" situation where one of you is working with 17 indicators and someone else is working with 14 etc etc.

> But you are right – if this tool is going to work for you on the ground you need to include indicators that are relevant to your market sector, so within the 20 indicators there will be 15 that are common to all sectors and five indicators that you can tailor and select yourselves.
>
> Let's put this into effect now and review how we are doing at the sales meeting.
>
> Regards
> Sarah
> CEO

That's a great outcome for all isn't it? Sarah involved her team members in the decision that was going to affect them but ended up with a key account management tool that could be monitored and scored in a similar way across their very different automotive, logistics, pharmaceutical, FMCG and aeronautic markets.

HEALTH CHECK QUESTIONS:

1. Today, how many of your key accounts see you as a partner?

2. Which twenty partnership indictors are right for you and what are the scores for each of your top key accounts?

3. In the future, which key accounts would you like to see move to "partner" status?

4. Which key accounts want to preserve a "master and slave" relationship and keep you as a supplier?

5. Is it time to "manage out" some accounts who do not work in the way that you want them to?

CONCLUSIONS:

- When key account managers work as partners, they understand that their job revolves around a very simple job description .... improving their own profitability and performance by improving the <u>customer's</u> profitability and performance.

- If you work as a partner you understand that you are in the financial services business with a black and white goal – i.e. putting some black and white on the <u>customer's</u> bottom line

- If you are an expert in the customer's world, you never have to sell again. Doors just keep opening as a result of the great work that you are doing and the great value you are adding

- The winners in the next decade, and those with the greatest chance of success will be companies who know more about their customers and their needs than the customers know themselves

- KAM is essentially a soft relationship issue. However, for those of you who believe that "what gets measured gets done", you will be pleased to hear that working with Partnership Indicators also produces a simple one-page KPI

- Strategically, if your business is in the top right quadrant of the matrix and your competitors are in the other three quadrants, that is the safest, most profitable, happiest place to be. For some of your competitors that will be "game over" ....if you can maintain your Partner position!

Tip three: Add value, not cost

There are only two types of organisations today - those that add value to their customers and those that add costs. Which type of organisation are you?

Companies that just add costs get hammered with comments like "How much – you must be joking!" and many struggle and go under. Companies that add value are in a different place, of course. If there is tangible evidence that customers are receiving plenty of ongoing value, then companies will survive and grow. All of this is obvious, when you think about it ....but many companies just don't think about it. As we said before, common sense is not necessarily common practice.

HEALTH CHECK QUESTIONS

1. If your company was arrested and charged with "adding value to key account customers" would there be enough evidence to convict it?

2. How does your company track and measure the value it creates?

3. Are you adding value in the key account's boardroom? (If not, you are probably "lower down the tree" and just seen as a commodity.)

4. Which aspects of your offering do key accounts truly value and which aspects are they unmoved by?

5. If your business ceased to exist today, what would key account customers miss about it tomorrow?

So, what can you do that will add value to your key accounts? Whilst working with our clients, we have seen some great ideas over the years:-

- Help the key account customer become more profitable - help them reduce costs and/or increase sales
- Help them find ways of staying in front of their customers
- Suggest joint R&D
- Give extra advice for free
- Send them useful articles and press cuttings
- Help them develop their future goals and strategies
- Turn your key decision makers into heroes - let them take the credit for your ideas
- Anticipate and solve their future problems
- Give them some business or a lead
- Introduce the key account to your customers/suppliers/network
- Give them a free place on your courses
- Sponsor their social event or conference
- Create social media networking or best practice groups for key people within your key accounts
- Help a key contact achieve a personal goal
- Help a key contact find a new job
- Be there when they need you

So, if your organisation is adding value you will receive (or be able to ask for) some testimonials from your happy major customers. But what would a "dream testimonial" look like? Let us introduce you to the Value Staircase.

```
4 | PRICELESS
3 | AUDITABLE
2 | QUANTIFIABLE
1 | IDENTIFIABLE
```

The best way to make this management-speak come alive is to give you an example. Imagine that one of your happy customers says this about you………………………

"When we first started to use your company, we were very impressed by the time you took to really understand our business (IDENTIFIABLE VALUE). Within 3-6 months a number of KPIs started to improve, including a 10% improvement in production ratios and a 24% improvement in our delivery time (QUANTIFIABLE VALUE). By the end of the first year the numbers were a no-brainer and we experienced a great return on our investment (AUDITABLE VALUE). But more than that, we now regard you as a valuable and trusted partner and have no hesitation recommending you to others (PRICELESS VALUE)."

One of our healthcare clients in Yorkshire decided to launch a new product range and 1 March was scheduled as the launch date. During the previous year, they piloted the new product range in Scotland and Yorkshire and were able to prove, and independently verify, that there was a 5:1 return on investment, within 6-9 months.

When the product went "live" and was rolled-out across the country, the total ROI for the NHS was estimated as being £11,143,000 and was broken down into six key savings areas:-

> 1. Increased speed of discharge from hospital = £1,730,000 saved
> 2. Reduced unplanned hospital admissions = £3,340,000
> 3. Reduced care home admissions = £3,420,000
> 4. Reduced number of carer sleepover nights = £557,000
> 5. Reduced home visit checks = £1,796,000
> 6. Other savings = £300,000
>
> The 5:1 return on investment is key here. That's not a difficult sale is it? It is like saying to the customer "Give me £1000 now and I will give you £5000, but I will have to post-date the cheque for 6-9 months' time!"
>
> The healthcare company, led by a brilliant visionary CEO called Jon, planned and built such a compelling "auditable" proposition that the new product launch exceeded all that had gone before by 75%!
>
> But as we said before, sitting above any auditable measurement sits the word "priceless."
>
> The key account was also able to give them a "Wow testimonial" that finished with the words "..........and we now regard your organisation as a dotted-line member of our team and would not dream of making a major strategic decision without consulting you first. You have transformed our organisation and we look forward to our ongoing partnership."
>
> Priceless!

You can ask for a testimonial at any time, of course, but sometimes they are easier to obtain at the end of a project, the end of the customer's business year or as a result of carrying out a Key Account Audit (covered in the next chapter).

When you ask for a testimonial don't be surprised if your request is greeted with a "Errr........yes.........we could do that for you."

Then as the customer glances at their watch, they will probably say "Tell you what..........I have got a lot on my plate. Why don't you write the testimonial and I'll sign it off?" This response is great news as it gives you an opportunity to write the testimonial following the Value Staircase model.

But don't be gushing and cheesy - tell an interesting but realistic story, with levels of value increasing over a period of time. One of the mistakes that companies often make is that they produce testimonials containing outrageous claims ....people look at them and think "They have paid someone to come out with that rubbish!"

In our own quest for testimonials, we recently asked two major customers if they would be happy to support us and provide one. Both asked us to write it, so they could sign it off, so we sent the two customers a tailored paragraph which we thought summarised the work we had carried out for each of them.

The first customer sent back an email saying "I could not have put it better myself!" The second phoned us up and said "I would never use the term "exceeding expectations"........in conversation I would say "go the extra mile." If you put that in, I will sign it off. Do you need my mugshot?"

Remember to check the dates on your testimonials. There is little value in publishing testimonials from years ago. It would be rather like a hotel proudly boasting "Customer Service Award Winner 2012." You would think "What on earth have they been doing since then!?"

Consider producing some video testimonials. They don't have to be professionally filmed in a studio. In today's world, video testimonials recorded on a mobile phone can still have great impact.....because they are interesting and "real".

To summarise then, testimonials have never been more important as they offer proof -they provide evidence that what you are saying is true. But sadly, in our world today, trust levels have dropped considerably due to a number of factors. Following the 2008 financial crisis, companies became more risk-averse. They no longer trusted one of their people to make major decisions - they created decision making processes that often consisted of 2-4 people.

But it is deeper than that. Sadly, in society, our trust levels have been shattered due to a number of high-profile stories in the media. You know who these people are but let us name a few..........priests, nuns, TV presenters, doctors, Hollywood directors, politicians and sports coaches etc etc.

You know the stories and we don't need to cover the details. Let's just say that groups of people we used to trust are no longer trusted. We have become more cautious and suspicious.

Back to the business world.............in the sales and account management process, trust is an important issue today. So, when your proposal or presentation is in front of a major prospect, who are they going to believe?

You, saying how wonderful your organisation is?

OR

Happy customers saying how wonderful you are?

Prospects thinking of working with you will trust your customer's words and that's why organisations need relevant, compelling "Wow!" testimonials for each of their target markets.

CONCLUSIONS:

- Be haunted by the question "If we ceased to exist today what would customers miss about us tomorrow?"

- If you gave a testimonial a job description you would be asking it to do one thing............provide <u>proof</u>.

- Make buying decisions easy by creating a library of interesting and relevant testimonials for each of your target markets or product groups. Remember that you will also need testimonials that are tailored to the interests and needs of key decision-makers.

    For example, a Finance Director will want to read about the return on investment, a Sales Director will want to read about how your solutions will impact on his/her customers and a HR Director will be interested to learn about the people-implications of going ahead with your organisation

- During regular review meetings ask your key accounts "what do we do for you that you particularly value?" and "what could we do to create more value for you in the future?"

- Get your happy customers to do the selling for you - testimonials should create an imaginary experience for others that is so compelling that it motivates them to also want to experience it.

Tip four: Build your business from the "outside-in"

From time to time organisations need to establish if the service they are providing is meeting and exceeding their key accounts' expectations. This is a BFO of course (blinding flash of the obvious) but, surprisingly, many companies do not have a process that proactively researches their key accounts to establish exactly how they feel.

Years ago, customers were researched via questionnaire and telephone, but today web-based survey tools are very popular and effective. But when thinking of a relatively small number of 5-20 key accounts something quite different is needed. At least once a year, these accounts need a face to face "Key Account Audit" to do the obvious thing i.e. say "thank-you for your business, we really appreciate it!" but also to establish how these important customers feel about the service they have received during the last 6-12 months.

This Key Account Audit also provides a great opportunity for CEOs and senior Directors to re-establish contact with their "opposite number" decision makers and have an important "strategic" dialogue about the future. So, when an organisation's "big guns" are deployed to carry out these Key Account Audits, they lead the KAM process for a period of time and then hand back the "implementation" phases to their account managers and colleagues. When we work with CEOs, we often say that key account management starts at the top………. or it doesn't start!

Fortunately, introducing the idea of a Key Account Audit to a key account customer is a very easy thing to do as it is very customer-friendly.

This is how an account manager called Karen "sold it in" to one of her key accounts in Colchester..................

> "As you know, Les, you are an important key account for us and we want to make sure that we are always exceeding your expectations and are in tune with how your business is changing and developing.
>
> So, from time to time our Directors carry out Key Account Audits with key decision makers and influencers and I know that my boss, Terry, is keen to meet you and your two colleagues in March.
>
> Terry's PA will be in touch to arrange those three appointments with you. These audits usually take 30-40 minutes each and please be open and honest in your feedback, including how you feel about the support you get from me.
>
> We value your business and the partner status that we currently enjoy. We have worked hard to earn it and we want to learn and improve in order to retain your business and support in the future etc etc"

Key account audits should be conducted with decision-makers and decision-influencers individually, not together. If you put three-four people in the same room at the same time you usually end up with a grey soup of rank and politics. Some people then talk a lot and others don't talk at all.

Key account audits need to be conducted with individuals as each person will have different experiences and expectations. To encourage some thought and discussion before the audit takes place, you can get the ball rolling with a good confirmation letter.

Back to account manager Karen and her key account customer. This is the email that was sent by Karen's boss Terry i.e. the person who would be conducting the audit.

Dear Les,

I am looking forward to meeting you at 10:00 on 23rd at your office, or at the Marriott if that is more convenient.

I am keen to discuss any aspect of our work and relationship with your company but in particular we are keen to learn:-

- During the last six months, where have we met your expectations?
- Where have we exceeded your expectations?
- Where have we fallen short?

Thank you for finding the time in your busy schedule to meet me. As you will know from Karen, we want to learn, listen and improve and your feedback will allow us to add more value to your company during the months and years ahead.

I look forward to seeing you soon.

Regards

Terry
CEO

PS. Separate meetings with Mitesh and Alan have also been arranged for 11:00 and 12:00.

So, let's have a look at some Key Account Audit questions. They should not be viewed as a script - they are a menu which can be "picked and mixed".

The questions below were produced as a result of our work with a CEO in West Bromwich called Denis. We were delighted to see that he decided to show some leadership on the key account agenda by carrying out the first ten audits.

The ten key accounts were huge - they contributed 75% of his sales and 52% of his profits. As he put it "If one of these key accounts went down, we would be in serious trouble - I am keen to learn more about the facts, the figures and their feelings."

Interestingly, Denis had plenty of KPIs in place monitoring the facts and the figures but was nervous about his customers' feelings. Although the KPIs suggested that all was well, feedback from his customer service team suggested that many important customers were not happy. Denis decided to investigate.

Here are his ten Key Account Audit questions:-

1. When you think of our service during the last six months, where have we met your expectations?
2. Where have we exceeded your expectations?
3. Where have we fallen short?
4. What unresolved issues are there?
5. How do we compare to other companies you use - both in our sector and all others?
6. How would you sum us up in a sentence?
7. How do you measure the contribution we make to your business?
8. Do you see us as a supplier or partner?
9. If we were an animal or bird, what would we be?
10. Overall, how many marks out of ten would you give us today?

At this point, we should point out that Denis did not want to ask the animal/ bird question, but we suggested that he should include it. He said "If you think I am going to ask that question, you can think again!" To be honest, he didn't actually use those words - we won't go into details of what he actually said................but the second word was "....off!"

But we eventually persuaded him to include that particular question and wished him well on his journey of discovery. Denis decided to carry out one key account audit each month, so ten months or so later, we met up with him again to see how he was doing.

We didn't record the conversation but the essence of it is outlined below (and Denis has since approved and "signed-off" the words you are about to read).

Phil: Hi Denis. How are you?

Denis: Good, Phil, thank you. I suppose you want to know about those key account audits I've been carrying out?

Phil: Yes, please. How did they go?

Denis: Fantastic. You would not believe the stuff we have dug out. In particular, all sorts of issues around our service, not just here in West Brom but also at our Parts Centre.

But I also identified loads of sales opportunities and many of these were completely unknown to my sales team.

Phil: So, you are a happy man, then?

Denis: I certainly am. In the future we are going to carry out key account audits well beyond the top ten customers and I'm also going to involve other members of the Board, including our Production Director.

Phil: Really, how did he react to that? I seem to remember you saying that he wasn't from "planet customer."

Denis: That's why he is one of three Directors now doing these audits. Without me rubbing his nose in it, he has been forced to face up to the performance of his factory and the late delivery issue. He will hear things he needs to hear.

Phil: That's a clever strategy, Denis. Basically, you have got him closer to the customer in a way that's not going to publicly embarrass him.

Denis: Yes, and my FD will also be out there doing some audits. I suspect that he will be listening to a few painful stories of major customers complaining about his team putting them on "stop".

Phil: So well done on all of that, Denis ....how did you get on with the "animal or bird question" you didn't want to ask?

Denis: Ah!

Phil: What does "Ah!" mean?

Denis: I need to thank you for that question as it was the single most revealing question I asked. Across the ten key accounts I asked about 38-40 people that question and 65% of them named the same animal.

Phil:..........and what was the animal?

Denis: The elephant.

Phil: Is that good or bad?

Denis: It could be good, bearing in mind those beasts are supposed to be intelligent, friendly animals, but on this occasion comparing my business to an elephant was a bloody disaster!

Phil: What exactly did the 65% say?

Denis: Here, read it for yourself. This is the final report. You will love the comment "Your business is like an elephant because it is slow, lumbering, can't change direction quickly and every now and again your people crap on us from a height!"

Phil: I see......but at least now you know how they feel. I suspected you might hear something like that – that's why I wanted you to include the question.

Denis: Although I said it was a bloody disaster, it has since improved things at this end.

Phil: How do you mean?

Denis: Well, firstly it really affected my people. They were devastated by all of the elephant comments – it got them at an emotional level – but I was quite pleased about that. If they are affected emotionally, they are more likely to think about it and then do something about it aren't they?

Phil: True, Denis. We believe that if customer feedback is shared in a timely and appropriate manner it will probably be the most important change-agent you can lay your hands on. Your people won't ignore it because it could affect their job security.

Denis: Exactly. You might be interested in something else I did..........I went off to Twycross Zoo, which is fifteen miles down the road from my house and bought 85 plastic elephants like this.

Phil: What a great day for the shop assistants. You must have made their day! What did you do with the 85 elephants?

Denis: In the canteen, as part of my monthly team briefing, I presented them to each member of staff..........starting with the Directors

Phil: What did you say?

Denis: I told them that if they had an office, I expected to see the elephant on their desk and that if they were driving a fork lift or truck, I expected to see the elephant taped on, in front of them somewhere.

Phil: So, overall, it sounds as if this piece of theatre on your part has caused the reaction you wanted it to?

Denis: Bloody right it has! But hats off to my people. One of the lads from the factory stopped me mid-sentence at one point and shouted out "So what animal should we be, boss?" That's a very fair question so we are going to be discussing that at the next team briefing.

Phil: So, when we are talking to other CEOs, is there anything else you would be happy for us to share, based on your experiences of carrying out these key account audits?

Denis: Yes, there is. Firstly, I would like to say that my key accounts loved these audit meetings because they were talking about their stuff and they were able to get a few things off their chests. There was certainly no resistance to the process at all.

Secondly, I would like to point out that although I set off with the ten questions you and I worked on together there was an interesting point in many of the meetings, maybe 30-40 minutes in, when the customer leaned over, with coffee pot in hand, and said "Would you like another coffee, Denis?"

Phil: ....meaning what......that they were enjoying talking to you and were happy to extend the meeting?

Denis: Exactly. So, I used these "second cup of coffee" moments to change gear. Having invested some time talking about our service performance and the past, I decided to ask some questions about them and their future. You won't have seen these questions before. You can have a copy if you like?

Phil: Yes please, Denis. And presumably these ten are another menu of questions, like the first ten questions? You didn't ask all of them?

Denis: Correct. Typically, I would ask 6-7 maybe. Here is the list.

1. How is your business changing and developing?
2. What pressures will you face in the future?
3. What are your top three objectives for the future?
4. How will you achieve them?
5. How could we help you achieve them?
6. Where could we add more value?
7. What do you see as being the big issues for our future relationship?

8. What would we have to do to score 10 out of 10 in the future?
9. Where would you be happy to see us have more of your business?
10. Is there anything else I need to know?

Phil: Thanks for that, Denis. David and I are also writing a book – can we use these?

Denis: Sure............but remember to send me the cheque!

Phil: Moving on quickly..............what sort of reaction did you get to the "where would you be happy to see us have more of your business" question?

Denis: It was both fascinating and worrying. It was as if the customers were putting a bloody great signpost in front of my eyes saying "If you put in a proposal for this part of our business (pointing) we would be happy to look at it............but we are never going to give you that part of our business (pointing in the other direction)".

Phil: Don't tell me...............your account managers were going in the wrong direction?

Denis: Sadly, yes. They were pursuing huge chunks of unwinnable business, often due to their egos, I suspect. What they should have been doing was listening to the customer and inviting him or her to point out the line of least resistance!

Phil: Just returning to the first bank of questions for a moment, were there any occasions when you thought you might be taking the lid off and opening up a real can of worms with a dissatisfied customer?

Denis: I wasn't worried about that. There is nothing the customer can say that is going to be damaging. Even bad news is a source of learning isn't it? The damaging thing would be if the customer says they are unhappy and fed up with us.............and we don't hear it!

Phil: Very true Denis. Thank you. We will put that in the book too.

CONCLUSIONS:

- You have heard this before.......... "their perception becomes your reality"

- We need to create a safe environment for the customer where things that need to get said...........get said!

- Customers don't care how much you know as long as they know how much you care

- If you listen very carefully, customers will explain your business to you.

- Problems are opportunities in disguise!

Tip five: Create the XX Factor

Let's re-introduce the three-legged stool model. As the diagram suggests, you can't get a three-legged stool to stand up on two legs – all three legs have to be strong and effective otherwise the stool will fall over.

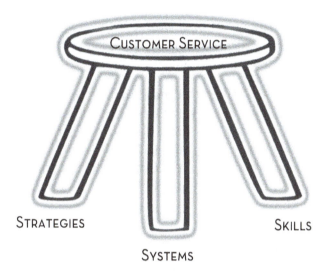

Here are some real-life examples of horror stories and happy stories that we have experienced in our lives as customers and consumers:-

1.Strategy horror story

Whilst staying at a hotel in London we went to Reception after an enjoyable evening meal and attempted to give them some future bookings.

Them: "Sorry, you will have to talk to our reception team from 0900 tomorrow"

Us: But we won't be here at 0900. We are checking out at 0800.

Them: Sorry!

What a bonkers idea – there we were confronted by a strategy that prevented us and other customers from providing them with future revenue. (By the way, we went elsewhere!)

1.Strategy happy story

When we checked out of the Fistral Beach Hotel in Newquay we were given goody bags containing bottled water, nuts, a banana and biscuits.

Bearing in mind the lengthy journey time that most guests would experience, that is a great strategy on the part of the hotel. Needless to say, we always stay at the Fistral Beach Hotel when we are working with our client down there............and are happy to recommend them to you, as you can see. We, as their happy customers, are happy to do the selling for them.

2.Systems horror story

Think about the plague of impersonal, computerised booking systems that throw you out if you are not quick enough, or those dreadful telephone answering systems where you are kept waiting for 25 minutes – we need say nothing more!

2.Systems happy story

David once ordered some IT equipment online and was delighted to find that the "system" told him that as his cumulative orders over a three-year period now totalled more than £250, he would be given an additional gift worth £25. Great customer service........... from the system.

3.Skills horror story

Phil, his wife and a friend went to a restaurant on the shores of Rutland Water and were disappointed to find that, upon arrival, they appeared to be "invisible" and were ignored. Eventually they were taken to a table and, forty minutes later, their drink and food orders were finally taken. The friend, Claire, then spoke to the waiter:-

Claire: Could I have ordinary mash with my main course please, instead of the celeriac mash?

Waiter: (shrugging) I'm not sure about that

Claire: Really? Is that a problem?

Waiter: I don't know - I haven't spoken to the chef yet!

This is not a strategy or systems issue - it is a skills issue - and clearly the waiter doesn't have the skills, or if he does, he can't be bothered to use them.

3.Skills happy story

David had a terrible motorway journey that featured numerous traffic problems and delays. He eventually arrived at his hotel at 11.30pm, looking completely frazzled. As he approached the smiling receptionist, he hoped that "check-in" would not take long and that he would soon be making a cup of tea in his room.

Receptionist: Good evening - you must be Mr. Ventura?

David: Yes, I am.

Receptionist: I know it's late, so why don't I take your bags to your room and arrange for some refreshments to be sent up? We can do the paperwork later. You can either pop back in half an hour or we can do it first thing in the morning.

Now it's time for us to put our "critical friend" hat on again and ask you some more questions.

HEALTH CHECK QUESTIONS

1. Marks out of ten for your service strategies?

2. ....and your service systems?

3. ....and the service skills of your people?

4. How would your colleagues answer the questions above?

5. How would your key accounts answer the questions above?

If you skipped the Introduction section of the book you will have missed the next couple of paragraphs. Customer service runs the same risks that exist in any relationship. Routine patterns of service become a habit, then assumptions are made and the habit becomes a rut, then the rut can sometimes become a cavern of arrogance and the unhappy customer decides to go elsewhere.

Did the dissatisfied customer bother to communicate their feelings at the time? No. Why? Well, nobody was listening to them anyway!

Over the years, many surveys have shown that only 9% approx. of customers switch suppliers due to "price" related issues but 68% of customers switch due to "perceived indifference." This doesn't mean that we don't care. It means that customers think we don't care.

But there is also a plus side to some of this research, which has shown that 75% of customers who had a complaint resolved to their total satisfaction were more loyal after the complaint than they were before it.

A major car manufacturer in the USA found that if a new owner brought their car in for a routine service and dropped the car keys at the desk saying "see you later" there was no meaningful, lasting relationship with the car owner.

However, if there was a major issue that then resulted in conversations with the salesperson, the service manager, the dealer principal and the mechanics then rapport, trust and meaningful, lasting relationships were created..........which led to a much higher number of owners remaining loyal and buying another of the company's vehicles further downstream.

We should point out, though, that within this story, resolving problems to the customer's <u>total satisfaction</u> was the key here.

So how do you create a customer-focused culture? Part of the solution is to make sure that you are employing talented people with the right attitudes, of course, but let's look at how you "engineer-in" effective customer-friendly processes to ensure that the customer is always delighted with what you are doing.

We will start by encouraging you to think of your own experiences as a customer i.e. when you are on the receiving end of customer service in a shop, hotel, online or on the phone. Think of a happy story and the joy when you received fantastic service. You probably told many of your friends. Or think of a horror story and the misery of experiencing appalling service which resulted in you telling all of your friends, relatives and social media networks.

So, what makes "brilliant service" brilliant? What makes "appalling service" appalling? What's happening in the head and the heart of the customer? Well, the scorekeeper at work here is the word EXPECTATIONS.

When you were on the receiving end of brilliant service, you got more than you expected and your <u>expectations were exceeded</u>.

When you were on the receiving end of appalling service you got less than you expected and the service provider fell short of your expectations. The scorekeeper in any service relationship is how you are performing compared to the other person's expectations.

It actually goes deeper than that. The scorekeeper in <u>any</u> relationship, including those at home, is how you are performing compared to the other person's expectations. Relationships that are rich, with plenty of moments of magic and joy, are no accident. The couple are working hard, making sure that they exceed each other's expectations.

They know that love is a verb.

We've all seen or experienced relationships that get into trouble. It is often where the couple has stopped working at it, have started to make assumptions and have stopped talking. They are no longer listening – they are simply waiting to speak. Sadly, they are now falling short of each other's expectations.

One of the theories that underpins relationship management and effective customer service is the "strokes concept"……as in "different strokes for different folks" etc etc. Some strokes are delivered physically, i.e. where there is direct physical contact, and some are delivered mentally i.e. where there is no physical contact.

Some strokes will have a positive effect on the other person and some will have a negative effect. All will become clear in the matrix on the next page.

	NEGATIVE	POSITIVE
PHYSICAL	Punch Kick Slap Push Inappropriate touching	Holding hands Peck on the cheek A kiss Hand on the arm Pat on the back
MENTAL	Swearing Criticism Sarcasm Silence Scowling	Compliment Recognition and praise Smile Humour "I love you!"

Top Left: Hopefully, there are none of these negative physical strokes going on in your relationships at home with friends and family. (By the way, when you relate this concept to the workplace, if there are negative physical strokes going on you might need to find a good lawyer!)

Top right: Positive physical strokes are very important to us and we all know the value and effect of holding hands or a tender, loving kiss. Interestingly, pensioners living on their own, or isolated prisoners in a cell, can often experience poor mental health due to the lack of positive physical strokes.

Bottom left: Negative mental strokes are painful. Being on the receiving end of criticism is, for most of us, an unhappy experience which we remember for a long time. The "scars" take a long time to heal.

Sometimes people deliver a sarcastic remark thinking that it is amusing, but for the other person it often lands differently. In the moment, it is often difficult to handle and upon reflection it is easy to interpret it as form of cowardly, veiled criticism.

Bottom right: These positive mental strokes provide the magic and joy in a relationship. If delivered in a genuine, meaningful way those "thank you" or "well done" or "you look beautiful tonight" moments are very precious and worth their weight in gold.

There is one other interesting dimension to the Strokes concept. Imagine that it is your birthday and your other half gives you a birthday card. It will be appreciated, but it probably won't score mega-points..............because you expect to receive it. The bigger issue will be if your partner forgets to give you a birthday card. So, the positive mental stroke produces few points, but the negative mental stroke produces a massive number of minus points.

But imagine that during the day your partner phones you and says "Guess what? I have booked a table at your favourite restaurant tonight. I will drive so that you can enjoy a few glasses of wine." This positive mental stroke will probably score mega-points......because it is unexpected. The effect of it will also last for months. So, there you have it. That is what Service PLUS+ is all about. People need to be trained to deliver Positive, Lasting, Unexpected Strokes.

Sometimes life can be so cruel. Research suggests that one negative stroke is so powerful that is takes five positive strokes to make up for it. The data also suggests that if a customer receives a negative stroke, they will tell at least 8-9 people about it but if they receive a positive stroke, they will only tell 4-5 people about it.

The arrival of social media probably means that, today, in the event of a negative experience a customer might tell their whole network about it! Reputational damage can often be swift and permanent.

So, let's look at the same matrix but, this time, with the customer service implications in the four boxes.

	NEGATIVE	POSITIVE
PHYSICAL	Limp handshake Inappropriate touching Bumping into someone	Firm handshake Peck on the cheek (if appropriate) Sympathetic hand on arm or shoulder
MENTAL	Turning up late Looking scruffy Avoiding eye contact Inappropriate tone of voice Losing customer's order details Eating whilst on the phone Blaming the system or a colleague Deflection e.g. "speak to Kerry, not me!" Saying "that's not my fault" Broken promises Delays during telephone calls Being too familiar e.g. "yes mate!" Nobody in reception Spelling customer's name incorrectly Asking the customer to phone back Bluffing and being caught out	Welcome board to greet the customer Using names to build rapport Showing genuine interest Recognising the voice on the phone Remembering peoples' small details Taking responsibility Phoning to warn of a likely problem Very fast response Compliments Praise Remembering the customer's birthday Going the extra mile Sending a free gift A follow-up phone call Positive language e.g. "we can sort that" Handwritten note on a compliment slip Under-promise and over-deliver

Let's look at how you would "engineer-in" brilliant and consistent customer service across your business. A good example (and one that most of us can relate to) is the hotel industry. Imagine that you have bought a hotel and that your vision is to become famous for customer service. Not just good at it – you want to be <u>famous</u> for it and acknowledged as the leader in your field. One of the first things that you would probably do with your new team would be to break down the customer's experience into bite-size pieces. Maybe something like this: -

1. **Enquiry stage** – a potential customer might check out the hotel on Trip Advisor, look at your website or phone you up.

2. **Check-In** -the next stage would be when the customer arrives at your hotel, parks their car and heads for reception.

3. Having checked in, they then head for **the room**.

4. **Bar and Restaurant** - later that evening, they might be in your hotel (hopefully) rather than visiting another bar and restaurant down the road

5. After a good night's sleep, they would return to reception to **check out**.

   That's a very simplified version of reality, but for illustration purposes it will suffice. Having identified the stages of the customer's journey, the next thing your hotel management team would do is to look at what typically happens in each of the five stages above. The word "typically" means what your competitors are doing.......not what you are going to do.

   You would then work with your team to develop the XX Factor i.e. in each stage of the customer's journey you need you would find ways of exceeding expectations.

Here is an example of what we mean, applied to stage one...........the Enquiry stage.

Typical experience (what your competitors do)	XX Factor (what you would do to exceed expectations)
Polite and friendly staff Take down some details Confirmation within 24 hours	Very polite and friendly staff Use the customer's name frequently Ask questions e.g."was there any particular reason why you were interested in that weekend?" and "what sort of things were you planning to do or see?" and "are there any special needs we need to be aware of?" As a result of questions above, offer to book venues, taxis or send details/weblinks etc Say that you are looking forward to welcoming them Immediate confirmation of booking

The rather dull but typical "industry average" six-out-of-ten experience on the left is passive. Competitor hotel staff simply take down details and don't proactively investigate the needs. On the right (i.e. at your hotel) you have trained your staff to investigate in a friendly and appropriate way so that they can influence the quality of the customer's downstream experience and exceed expectations.

For example: -

1. If the customer tells your staff that the reason why they want to come to the hotel is that it is their wedding anniversary that weekend you could then arrange for a card to be put in their room with a small bunch of flowers or present them with two glasses of complimentary champagne when they go to the bar

2. If the customer tells your staff that they are keen to go to an outdoor music festival, you could give them a packed lunch or in the event of bad weather send them on their way with one of your hotel umbrellas

3. If the customer tells your staff that they are recovering from a leg operation you could arrange for them to have a ground-floor room close to reception and make sure that someone carries their bags for them

There are a couple of very interesting things about the suggestions and ideas in the right-hand XX Factor column. They don't cost pounds, they cost pennies and they don't take hours to deliver, they take a few seconds to deliver. The extra thought that goes into developing the XX Factor column makes good business sense. Profitability increases as a result of customers receiving exceptional service delivered by exceptional people.

CONCLUSIONS:

- KAM is a lot like tennis – those that don't serve well, lose!

- In today's world, just meeting expectations is not enough. The difference between ordinary service and extraordinary service is that little bit extra

- When you service your key accounts, you need to deliver Service PLUS+ ....positive, lasting, unexpected strokes

- It takes months to find a customer but seconds to lose one

- We make no apologies for repeating the "First Rule Of Business" – look after your major customers before someone else does!

Tip six: Become an expert in their world

Remember the challenge from chapter two in this book...........i.e. if a key account customer asked you to deliver a short presentation on your understanding of their business, could you do it ....etc etc?

Maybe a simple, one-page understanding of the key account's business showing where they are now, where they are going in the future, how they intend to get there and the role you could play in that journey would help?

Have a look at the diagram below. Although it is tempting to get immersed in the details, try not to do that. It is the structure of the diagram that we want to draw your attention to. This was one of our key accounts a couple of years ago. We needed to understand exactly what was going on in the customer's world, before we found ourselves pitching to them in their board room.

1. Down the left-hand side of the diagram, in the TODAY column, is a ten-point summary of where the key account is today.

2. Down the right-hand side of the diagram, in the FUTURE column, is a ten-point summary of where the key account wants to be in the future. The word "future" can mean anything, but in this particular example it means two years.

3. So, in order to get from the left to the right over a two-year period, the key account has four main "strategic bridges" in place...... i.e. CUSTOMERS, SERVICES, PEOPLE AND SYSTEMS. You don't have to have four strategies, of course, but in this example the customer happens to have four.

    The lowest number of strategies we have ever seen is two and the highest is eight, which is not surprising really, as these are the major business processes at work here.

4. Sitting within each of the four strategies are a number of projects. For example, the Services strategy has three projects going on................i.e. Technology Products, Life Cycles and Integrated Solutions. At this stage of our explanation, you might be thinking "where on earth did that information come from?" Well, if you are talking to the right people at the right time and asking the right questions in the right way and listening effectively, why wouldn't you have this level of understanding?

"A wise old bird sat on an oak. The more he saw, the less he spoke. The less he spoke, the more he heard. Why aren't we like that wise old bird?"

~ Edward Hersey Richards~

5. So now put yourself in our shoes. We checked out the accuracy of our Strategic Bridges diagram with some friendly and supportive allies within the account. Interestingly, they commented on a couple of areas that we had got completely wrong, but with their help we were then able to change our understanding before we found ourselves in the customer's board room where we knew that a couple of attendees were strongly in favour of giving the business to one of our competitors.

6. A diagram like this makes selling so much easier. All we had to do was to say "If we have understood your business correctly this is where you are today (left-hand column) and this is where you are going in the future (right-hand column). You have told us that you have four strategies in place to deliver your desired future and a number of projects going on in each one................which is very interesting because we can help you with five (shaded) areas.......Service Excellence, KAM, Culture, Communication and Succession." These were the areas where we then provided a range of consultancy, training and coaching services.

7. Interestingly, with this particular company, we also found ourselves saying "You have told us that Market Research and Recruitment are things you will need to look at in the future..........we don't provide either of those services, but we know people who do. Would you like us to connect you with them etc etc?" Not surprisingly, the customer jumped at the opportunity and really appreciated the extra value i.e. us saving them time, money and hassle.

8. You could say that the five shaded areas are the five "jigsaw pieces" that we were waiting to lay down and explain. You would be right. But the key point here is that we needed something else before we knew exactly when and how to play our jigsaw pieces...............

...we needed to understand the "picture on the box" of the jigsaw.......and that is what the Strategic Bridges concept is designed to do.

- Life is often about timing so let's look at the best times of the year to be having "Strategic Bridges conversations".

    You might want to build the diagram when you are trying to win the business in the first place (as it screams "we understand your world better than anyone else you will ever talk to!")

- You might want to build it if the ownership of the company changes and you need to be seen to be "starting again" with the new decision makers, rather than relying on your track record and past glories.

- In the case of a family business, you might want to build the diagram to assist the exit of the owners. For example, if the owners wanted to sell the business in five years' time, you could build the diagram as a five-year journey, not the two-year journey on our example.

- When building it with a major key account, you might want to facilitate an Annual Strategic Review, built around the start of the customer's new business year.

    There might be an action point here. Could your account managers tell you the dates of their key accounts' business years? How about a white board, or something visible on the system, that displays these key year-end/start dates well in advance?

- One of the advantages of using a label like "Annual Strategic Review" is that some senior decision-makers will attend the meeting due to the "strategic" nature of it. These could be people who have been avoiding your regular "routine" review meetings ....now delegated to managers lower down the tree.

You can have great fun with this concept. One of our clients in Warrington decided to carry out Annual Strategic Reviews with their top ten clients using an "away-day" format and seven of their clients agreed to do it. What a fabulous result for a first attempt. Imagine the scene............there they were, in a nice country hotel with plenty of coffee and biscuits, with three flip charts in the room representing the main components of the diagram. At the start of the meeting, only two flip charts were visible. On the left was the "Today" flip chart and on the right was the "Future" flip chart.

Once completed, our client moved the two flip charts apart and placed a third flip chart in the gap........i.e. the flip chart that would develop and record the strategy and projects that would become the middle of the diagram. Apparently, everyone enjoyed the meetings which were informal, friendly, laced with banter and with plenty of enthusiasm and goodwill. The meetings concluded with a light-bite and an early finish (which sounds like the perfect day, doesn't it?)

To summarise, would you want to build a Strategic Bridges understanding for each and every customer........no! But would you want to build this level of understanding for each of your top three, top five or top ten key accounts............absolutely yes, yes, yes!

CONCLUSIONS:

- If you are an expert in the customer's world you never have to sell again!

- Understand the 3Ps.....the customer's problems, pressures and priorities, then help them to find the right solutions (including yours!)

- You should have ideas and solutions to problems the customer doesn't yet know they have

- Customers are not really interested in your business – they are paying you to learn more about their own

- The only way to sell more of your products and services is to stop talking about your products and services............talk about their stuff!

Tip seven: Find the right round pegs

One of our CEO clients, Hannah, says that account management is "too important to be left to the sales team!" That statement is potentially offensive (particularly if you are an account manager) so let's quickly explain what Hannah means.

She is trying to draw the distinction between an average salesperson and an exceptional key account manager.

Average Salesperson	Exceptional Key Account Manager
Understands how to sell	Understands why customers buy
Looks at world through own eyes	Looks through the customer's eyes
Sees role as top-line	Sees role as bottom-line
Competitive glory-hunter	Collaborative team player
Has a plan	Understands their plans
Short-term tactician	Long-term strategist
Credible with 1-2 decision makers	Credible with everyone, at all levels
Subservient	An "equal"
Talker who waits to speak	Active listener who understands
Often irritating	Often inspirational
Expert in own stuff	Expert in the customer's stuff
Delivers standard pitch	Tailors language to customer
Believes that buyers are liars	Understands buyer motivation
Enjoys closing the customer	Enjoys opening-up the customer
Win-lose	Win-win
Sees objections as obstacles	Sees objections as interest
Overcomes objections forcefully	Handles objections skilfully
Worries about own targets	Helps customer hit their targets
Viewed with some caution	Seen as a trusted advisor
Customers tolerate them	Customers look forward to visits

So, you can see that she is interested in recruiting a very different type of sales animal and someone who fits the KASH Profile for the job i.e. someone who has the right knowledge, attitudes, skills and habits for the job.

On the next page, you will see the tool that she uses to ensure that she gets the round pegs in the round holes.

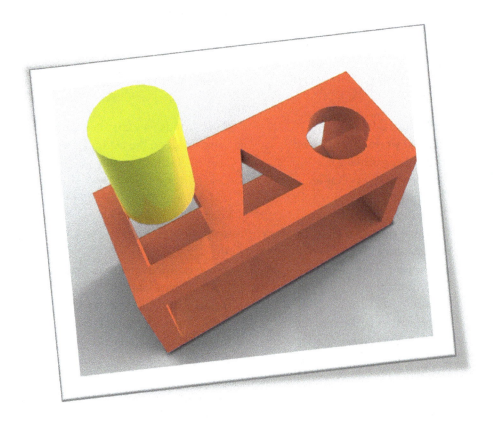

Knowledge

Customer's Strategies and Plans	1	2	3	4	5	6	7	8	9	10
Products / Services	1	2	3	4	5	6	7	8	9	10
Competitors	1	2	3	4	5	6	7	8	9	10
Own Structure, Processes Polices	1	2	3	4	5	6	7	8	9	10
Current and Likely Legislation	1	2	3	4	5	6	7	8	9	10
Business Planning	1	2	3	4	5	6	7	8	9	10
Customer Profile	1	2	3	4	5	6	7	8	9	10

Attitudes

Team Player	1	2	3	4	5	6	7	8	9	10
Genuinely Customer Focused	1	2	3	4	5	6	7	8	9	10
Well Rounded Outlook	1	2	3	4	5	6	7	8	9	10
Positive - Sees Solutions	1	2	3	4	5	6	7	8	9	10
Goal Orientation	1	2	3	4	5	6	7	8	9	10
Being a Catalyst for Change	1	2	3	4	5	6	7	8	9	10
Competitive Instinct	1	2	3	4	5	6	7	8	9	10
Strong and Resilient	1	2	3	4	5	6	7	8	9	10

Skills

Research and Planning	1	2	3	4	5	6	7	8	9	10
Questioning	1	2	3	4	5	6	7	8	9	10
Listening and Summarising	1	2	3	4	5	6	7	8	9	10
Presenting Tailored Solutions	1	2	3	4	5	6	7	8	9	10
Written Proposals and Letters	1	2	3	4	5	6	7	8	9	10
Negotiating	1	2	3	4	5	6	7	8	9	10
Internal Marketing / Persuasion	1	2	3	4	5	6	7	8	9	10
Organising and Running Customer Meetings	1	2	3	4	5	6	7	8	9	10
Networking Skills	1	2	3	4	5	6	7	8	9	10
Closing / Gaining Commitment	1	2	3	4	5	6	7	8	9	10

Habits

Punctuality	1	2	3	4	5	6	7	8	9	10
Well-Organised	1	2	3	4	5	6	7	8	9	10
Appearance	1	2	3	4	5	6	7	8	9	10
Ability to Make Things Happen	1	2	3	4	5	6	7	8	9	10

The shaded boxes on the profile are where the job holder (Bob, in this case) needs to be and the circled squares are where he feels he is as a result of a self-assessment exercise. The gaps become a training and development need and let's also not forget that Bob is well aware of how he learns best and will have some thoughts on how to close the gaps down. Would he learn best by going on a training course, or by accompanying a colleague on joint visits to witness the real world? Bob knows!

At the end of the day, it is his responsibility to close the KASH gaps down and in many ways, his job security depends on it. In a constantly changing business world, some KASH items will become more important (i.e. the green boxes move to the right), some will become less important (i.e. the green boxes will move to the left, some new items will be added every year and some will drop off the profile altogether.

So, do your people need the same KASH Profile or do they differ? For example, if you have someone managing an account with the MOD does s/he have the same profile as someone managing the Google or Virgin Atlantic account?

So, have you got the round pegs in the round holes i.e. the right people managing each key account? Here is an example of a company that got it badly wrong............................

> A few years ago, we were involved in a key account management project with a company based in Luton. The CEO, Andrew, popped his head into the training room and asked us to see him before we left at the end of the day.
>
> We went to see him and he explained that he was concerned about a poor-performing key account in Hull, which produced something like 20% of their revenue.

We went into our usual question-mode to establish the situation and during the discussion we asked Andrew who was managing the key account in Hull.

"That will be Sam, then" said Andrew, who then gave us a brief outline of Sam's background with the company. We then asked what we thought was a very basic question. "Why is Sam managing this particular key account?"

Andrew looked surprised and said "Well it's obvious. Sam is managing the key account in Hull because he............errr...............lives....................errr....................fairly close to Hull."

We looked equally surprised. "Are you really saying then, Andrew, that the main selection criteria for the person who is going to manage this important key account of yours in Hull is that they need to live ".......fairly close to Hull?"

Andrew said "Well, the key account is in Hull and Sam lives near Hull, so it's bound to be him isn't it? Wouldn't all companies work like that?"

"No, they wouldn't" we said.

We went on to explain that although there will always be a place for allocating smaller customers using regional borders and boundaries, when working with important key accounts companies should adopt "situational account management."

Perhaps an account manager living in Manchester, Birmingham or London might have been better qualified (i.e. KASH) to manage the key account in Hull! The round pegs should be in the round holes. The cost of the extra mileage has to be considered, of course, but it has to be compared to the extra value that the key account is going to receive and the extra profitability that will find its way onto your bottom-line.

We always try and practice what we preach. Some years ago, Phil was managing one of our key accounts in Walsall and, for a number of reasons, felt that a colleague called Martin would be better managing the account in the future.

So, Phil floated the idea with the customer who basically said "OK, that makes sense, but we need to meet Martin just to make sure that the rapport is there." In the weeks that followed, Martin did indeed visit the customer and became our account manager, with Phil still involved in a supporting role. We thought that made a lot of business sense and, needless to say, Martin then did a better job than Phil would have done........and that was exactly the point!

CONCLUSIONS:

- It's common sense, but have you got the round pegs in the round holes?

- The person managing the account should be the person who is best qualified to achieve the objectives you have for the customer and the person best qualified to achieve the objectives you have for your company.

- How does "situational account management" affect your world? Which account managers need to move? How will you convince your Key Accounts that this is a good move for them?

- When looking for new account managers, recruit for attitude and train for skills (not the other way around)

- Recruiting account managers is basically three "C" questions. "Are they able to do the job (COMPETENCE)?" "Will they love the job (COMMITMENT)?" and "Will they fit in (CULTURE)?"

Tip eight: Lead KAM as a team sport

This is the "leadership and culture" chapter. Clearly there are some huge implications here for CEOs and Directors – an organisation with high levels of motivation and employee engagement is going to deliver better levels of service excellence than an organisation that has de-motivated and disengaged people.

We believe that "CEO" stands for Chief Engagement Officer! We have worked with many different types of Chief Executive – some have built fabulous "passion centres" (rather than profit centres) and sadly others have built prisons for the human soul.

We believe that an important KPI that affects key account management is "heartcount" i.e. the % of people who have their hearts and minds emotionally caught up with what their company is trying to do. In an ideal world (which is where management consultants live of course!) the heartcount should match the headcount. If you are reading this thinking "That's fine in theory but I will do the people stuff once I have got the profitability sorted out" we would like to (politely) challenge your thinking.

> **There is a very simple definition of the word "profitability"**
>
> **................it is the downstream consequence**
>
> **of exceptional people delivering exceptional service!**

Let's leave it there as there are many excellent books, speakers and consultants you might already be familiar with in this leadership area.

We will return to the focus of this book and concentrate on the KAM side of the leadership and culture issue.

Key account management is a team sport. It is not a job for lone heroes who go where nobody has gone before, in pursuit of commercial glory. Key account management is, in many ways, part of everyone's job within the company. Looking at it simply, maybe there are only two groups of people within an organisation?

1. There is a group of people servicing the customer
2. There is another group of people who are providing an internal service to the group of people servicing the customer.

Here is the organisation chart developed and published by Kerry (CEO) and Bernard (Operations Director) - the two key people running a major printing business in Yorkshire. They promoted it, protected it and policed it and over an eighteen-month period it had a major impact on the development of their "one company" culture.

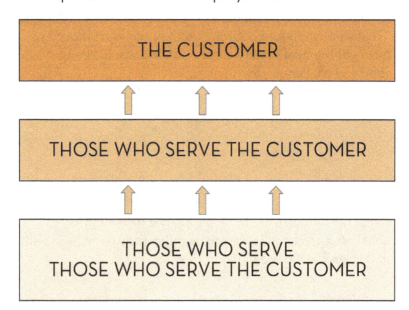

Back to an earlier reference to teamwork. Remember the Partnership Indicators in chapter two? One of them was "we have good multi-level relationships" but what does that actually mean?

In the diagram below, imagine that your organisation is on the left and the key account organisation is on the right. Within each organisation, there will be director-level decision makers at the top, managers in the middle and account management and support teams underneath them.

The dimensions of the pyramids are also fair and accurate. There are relatively few directors in organisations, many more managers and considerably more people in account management and customer support functions.

So, if you were to claim that you had "good multi-level relationships etc etc" the first thing you would expect to see is three levels connected with three levels. Although we would hope that there is synergy and understanding between the two, let's use conventional language for a moment and say that people are connected to their "opposite number."

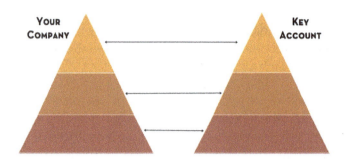

Many of these contacts would be face to face but maybe some would be communicating by telephone, Skype, emails or meeting up at corporate hospitality events.

But in reality, it is a little more complex than that, of course. Maybe three-four people within your organisation would be in touch with three-four people within the key account, so the two pyramids are more likely to look like this.

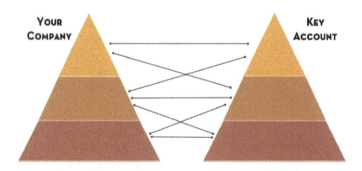

...............and if the situation above existed you would "tick" the Partnership Indicator. If two levels on your side were in contact with two levels within the key account, you would still be vulnerable so that would be a "cross" in Partnership Indicator terms. If one person on your side was in contact with all three levels within the key account, that would also be a cross.

Why? Because if your account manager left your organisation, they could take your customer with them.

Your T.E.A.M. should own the key account,

not the account manager

...............Together Everyone Achieves More!

Let's have a look at one of the most effective teams we have worked with. They have turned key account management into a team sport and gone to the top of their league.

Monday	Tuesday	Wednesday	Thursday	Friday
1	2	3	4 TEAM KAMDAY	5
8	9	10 SALES DIR AVAILABLE	11	12
15	16 TEAM KAMDAY	17	18	19
22	23	24	25	26 SALES DIR AVAILABLE
29 CEO K/A AUDIT	30 CEO AVAILABLE	31		

As you can see on our depiction of a typical working month for this team, there are two "KAM Days" where team members proactively help each other to convert new business opportunities, work on presentations, proposals, contract renewals and tenders etc. When they are out and about in the field if they want to call on the support of a colleague on a joint visit, they can confidently refer to a colleague in the discussion without having to ask them..........they know that the colleague is available.

At the end of a first meeting with a potential key account, the account manager's summary might sound something like this:

"When we meet again, I would like to introduce you to my colleague who has a lot of experience in these types of complex projects. I think you will find his thoughts on the subject very interesting and he has some great stories on how we have been able to help organisations like yours………..etc etc"

After the first meeting, the account manager would then send a quick text message to the colleague, which effectively would book him/her for the day. Job done.

You will see that the Sales Director has committed himself to two days in the field and he would be booked in the manner already described. However, in the real world, the Sales Director knows that he may have to cancel one of these days due to last-minute business pressures from key accounts and prospects. In this event, the second date in the diary becomes a Holy Day (as he calls it) and always happens.

The CEO, Cheryl, prefers to deliver her commitment to the team through two days, back-to-back. During the two days she supports and works with two-three members of her team. Activities typically include Key Account Audits and second visits to new prospects where there is a high probability of her presence helping to secure the business. Overnight, in a local hotel somewhere, she will probably see two-three more team members whilst enjoying a nice meal and a glass of wine. As the good book says, "teamwork makes the dream work!"

"It is not speeches at the moment of battle that render soldiers brave - the veteran scarcely notices and the new recruit will forget them at the first shot.

Speeches from leaders are only useful during the campaign - on the ground and in the trenches - doing away with poor motivation, correcting false information, improving morale and keeping a proper spirit alive in the camp!"

~ Napoleon ~

Here's another key account team, led by Adrian, in Chester. Adrian doesn't ask his team members to do their best........he asks them to do what they are best at. All members of the team sell all products to all market sectors, but he appoints "vertical champions" (the *s) who are called on, as and when needed.

Team	Food Sector	Transport & Logistics	Printing	Professional Services
Keith	✓	✓*		
Sheila		✓		✓*
Mike	✓		✓*	
Pat	✓*			

Put yourself in Keith's shoes - a relatively new member of Adrian's team with a background and expertise in the transport and logistics sectors (see asterisk above).

When he found himself getting to proposal stage with a major prospect in the professional services sector, he called on his vertical champion colleague, Sheila, to support him. During their presentation, Keith summarised the needs that had been identified earlier and Sheila presented their solutions using her considerable experience and a wide range of ideas and stories to clinch the deal.

But sometimes we come across companies that suffer from a little "creative tension" or, even worse, tribal warfare between departments and divisions. There is a very famous quote from the American writer, Rosabeth Moss-Kanter who said "The quality of service we give the customer is influenced by the quality of service we give each other"

So if you are managing a team of account managers and their various support colleagues across the business, there may be some occasions where you need to clear the air, examine how well the team is working and discuss actions that will improve internal relationships.....which will then influence external customer service.

Here is an exercise we developed when we worked with Adrian's team on one of its "away-day" training sessions near Knutsford.

We asked members of the team to (individually) identify which of the following teams they resembled and why, and which team they would like to resemble in the future and why.

A rugby team	A hockey team
A gang of criminals	The cast of a play
A human family	The Cabinet
The crew of a spacecraft	Staff of a school
'Apprentice' contestants	Fire crew at an emergency
Gold medal rowing crew	Soldiers on active service
Staff of operating theatre	A circus
A girl/boy band	Airline crew

Lively, amusing discussions identified, in every case, that team members could see that there was a gap between their current team behaviours and those of their dream team. Although they differed on the current state of affairs, they agreed that they would like to resemble the gold medal rowing crew. An action plan was built and, during the following six months, they moved closer to peak performance, "all pulling in the same direction etc"

The vision of the rowing team resonated so strongly that one team member suggested that they should hold all future meetings at a rowing club. A club with suitable meeting and catering facilities was then located and that's exactly what they did. Adrian told us that as soon as team members arrived at the rowing club's car park they were "in a different emotional state" and ready to "go for gold!"

In a similar vein, here is an exercise we used when we worked with Teri's team in London. Although she had attempted to clear the air at her previous sales meetings, there had been a subdued response, with team members choosing to withdraw and play it safe.

This exercise became known as the "dot-comm discussion" where team members completed a number of incomplete sentences and "joined up the dots."

During the last three months the high points for me were............

The low points were............

As a team we worked well together when............

We worked poorly when............

If we could put the clocks back, we should have............

In the future we need to do more............

and less............

My commitment to the team will be to............

This team can help me by............

Our team leader can help me by............

Our team motto in the future should be............

Teri's team members found that the exercise triggered deep emotions and feelings and, in the warm conducive environment created by Teri, they talked openly and honestly about issues that were happening in their world and the actions needed in the future. They did a little "storming" and then moved on to "performing."

People remained polite and courteous throughout and dealt with some difficult "stuff" in an adult and supportive way.

As a result, they created a nice one-liner that influenced their behaviour thereafter............... "Let's attack the problem, not the person!"

CONCLUSIONS:

- Your organisation should own the key account......not the account manager. Build relationships at all three levels

- Going over the head of a key contact is potentially dangerous – deploy Director "big guns" to have a strategic conversation, at their level, in the boardroom instead (Key Account Audit?)

- KAM team leaders need to create an environment where things that need to get said................get said!

- Individuals are imperfect, but teams can be perfect. They are often a collection of talented differences that share the same visions, values and goals. Don't fear criticism from team members. Your most negative no-man is more useful than your best yes-man.

- There will be many smaller customers where you will be happy for an account manager to refer to them as "my customers" but at key account level the phrase "my customers" is a serious offence..........it is about "our customers." To put it another way, key account management is about more "we" and less "me!"

Tip nine: Build KAMPlans

We can't remember who said it but there is a belief that there are three different types of people and organisations:-

1. Those that watch things happening
2. Those that make things happen
3. Those that wonder "what happened!?"

In order to make KAM things happen, we believe that there needs to be a user-friendly system and toolkit in place to proactively manage each key account. Some of our clients add these "KAMplan" toolkits to their existing CRM systems and other clients prefer to keep them well away from their CRM system. To quote Stuart, a CEO client of ours in Haywood, Lancashire, "we are not a great fan of fancy CRM systems ....they are where you lose things alphabetically!

So what does a good key account plan look like? The good news, you will be pleased to hear, is that it is remarkably simple and low-cost. (Sadly, some of our clients have spent a small fortune with major consultancies who installed full "bells and whistles" toolkits that didn't work in the real world).

These toolkits may have looked very impressive as part of a thesis or MBA course work, but in the real world they need to pass the "water cooler test" i.e. what account managers and their colleagues say, chatting by the water cooler when their bosses are out of the building. Maybe this is the dream conversation?

First account manager: "When we first started using this toolkit, I wasn't convinced it would add value, but it has been a great experience...

...and I probably wouldn't have won the business the other day had I not been through its very simple processes"

Second account manager: "Yes I've had that experience as well......for me, it has been a simple and effective coach that has made sure I have covered off all the bases. I'm going to roll-out the process to more of my key accounts".

So back to the key question - what should a good key account plan look like? How should it be structured? Imagine that one of your most successful account managers, Pat, has just won the National Lottery and is £8.5m better off. Over the weekend, it's been a tough decision for Pat (!) but she has decided to leave your organisation. She is leaving for the Seychelles clutching her £8.5m, never to be seen again.

After a congratulatory handshake, you then decide to say "Just a minute, Pat. As you are managing our top key account, which brings in more than a third of our business, we need a handover meeting before you disappear. At 4pm today, I will ask Warren to attend the handover meeting and I will also sit in to make sure I know what's going on."

Against this scenario, what would you expect the departing Pat to talk about? What information should be handed over? Some of this info might be on the CRM system. It might be on Pat's laptop or a hard-copy. It might, of course, be in the back of Pat's head, having failed to get on to the system?

What would be on your shopping list? If you would like to make a few notes there is some space below..............................

The Handover Shopping List	
? ? ? ? ?	? ? ? ? ?

We are going to bet that whatever you have included in your handover shopping list, it will fall into one of three blocks of content. We are confident that we can convince you that a good key account plan is essentially three key questions.......... or three key pages.......or three key screens of data.

Back to your departing key account manager, Pat, who has already started to say her "goodbyes" around the building. At the handover meeting, the first question you would ask Pat would bring together all the key pieces of INTELLIGENCE and it is as simple as "What is the current situation within this key account, Pat?"

The best way for Pat to reply, would be for her to use the SWOT language that has been around for decades and would tell you the strengths, weaknesses, opportunities and threats within the key account. You wouldn't want Pat to talk for forty minutes. You are interested in a small number of big points, so if she covered three-four points in each of the four SWOT areas you would probably be very happy with that.

The second question you would ask Pat is linked to her INTENTIONS and would sound something like "What are your future plans for this key account, Pat?"

So far, we have asked Pat about the INTELLIGENCE situation and her INTENTIONS ......the third and final area we need to look at is detailed IMPLEMENTATION i.e. "Finally then Pat, who needs to do what, by when?"

To summarise, here are those key questions and points in diagrammatic form:-

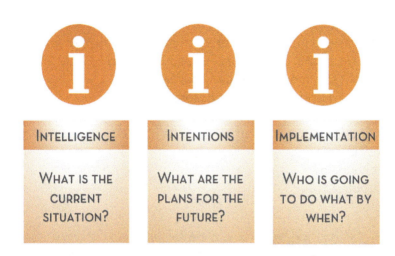

Think about your shopping list again. Quite a few of the items on your list are probably going to be in the INTELLIGENCE area e.g.

- Who are the key players within the key account?
- How does the decision-making process work?
- What do we know about the key peoples' likes and dislikes?
- What is the trading history for the last couple of years?
- How are we currently performing?
- How does the customer feel about our service?
- Have we hit our KPIs?
- What is known about competitor activity?
- Are there any outstanding issues or problems?
- Have any promises been made?

Here are ten simple, practical tools that we believe should be used to help build up a simple and accurate summary of the intelligence situation. Some we have already covered and others (the asterisks) we will look at shortly.

1. Company profile*
2. Partnership Indicators score out of 20 - already covered
3. Key Account Audit results - already covered
4. Recent testimonials - already covered
5. Strategic Bridges - already covered
6. Organisation chart **
7. Allies and Enemies matrix ***
8. Key personnel ****
9. Favours log *****
10. Supplier Split ******

*So, what would you expect to see on the Company Profile page? These vary from company to company, of course, but typically we would see this sort of thing..........................

Customer Name	Their markets
Address	Market share
Number of sites	Their major customers
Phone numbers	Their competitors
Website	Their current performance
Ownership of the company	Trend of their performance
Business year	Date contract commenced
Companies in the group	Contract renewal date
Landmarks in their history	Key contacts
Their products	Email addresses
Major brands	Mobile numbers
etc etc	etc etc.

Let's move on to the next asterisk

**These days, organisation charts are often visible on company websites but, if not, they are relatively easy to obtain. Many customers will simply press a button and print one off for you. You may also want to consider asking the customer to draw the organisation chart. This slows them down and as they draw it, they will probably tell you an interesting and revealing story about "who's who?" and why they are in that role. They might also tell you little pieces of gossip that might be quite useful to you.

How they draw the chart can also be quite revealing. Have a look at the two diagrams below. They are the same organisation, but you would get a feel for the author of the chart (the key decision maker) just by looking at how they have drawn their diagrams.

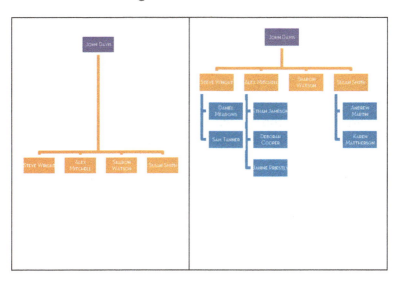

The diagram on the left represents someone who is 'status-driven' and not a 'people person'. The diagram on the right clearly suggests the opposite.

*** Let's have a look at the Allies and Enemies matrix.

	Harry Williams	Very Possitive Ally		
		Positive		Sue Jackson
		Interested		
Minor Decision Influencer	Major Decision Influencer		Minor Decision Maker	Major Decision Maker
Tom Chaudray		Indifferent		
		Negative		
		Very Negative Enemy		Dick Hall

As you can see, the matrix plots the level of authority and the level of positivity within the decision-making process. The horizontal axis features two levels of decision-influencing (on the left) and two levels of decision-making (on the right). The vertical axis features three levels of positive emotion (above the horizontal line) and three levels of negative emotion below it.

Imagine then, that these four people are going to decide if they are going ahead with a major proposal that your company has submitted/presented. Let's have a look at who's who around the table:-

Sue: She is a decision maker who is positive towards you

Harry: A very positive ally of yours (he loves you!) and on this particular project he is a major influencer. Maybe he is a decision influencer on the project because he has delegated it to Sue and Dick.

Tom: He is an indifferent decision influencer

Dick: Bit of a problem here. He is a major decision maker who is very anti or, as one of our clients put it................"Dick probably is one!"

So if this matrix was completed by Pat, your departing account manager who has just won the Lottery, and then presented to you and your colleagues at the handover meeting there are clearly a number of questions you might like to ask Pat:-

1. Do we know why Dick is so anti? (Is there a price issue? Has he had dealings with us before - did we let him down? Is there a chemistry issue?)
2. How do we "move him up the matrix" so he becomes more positive?
3. Can we leverage the relationship with Sue and Harry, so they influence Dick?
4. If this is a non-starter, can we move Tom up the matrix so that there are three people above the horizontal line?
5. How has Pat been spending the time?
- Sue: ? %
- Harry: ?%
- Tom: ?%
- Dick: ?%
6. When was the last time anyone met Dick?
7. Who else from our company knows these four people - does anyone have a good relationship with Dick?

8. How does the decision-making process work – who speaks to whom, in what order?
9. What is the probability of winning the business?
10. What will the matrix look like in twelve months' time and where should we be spending our time now?

Note - The Allies and Enemies Matrix plots the decision-making <u>process</u>, not just the people who are known. In the earlier stages of the relationship, if your account manager asked the question "Could I just ask how the decision making process works?" and Sue replied by saying "Tom and I draw up a short list of four-five possible suppliers, then we whittle them down to three and they then present their proposal to all four of us............... then we ask Alan in Brussels to rubber stamp it".

Then Alan in Brussels should be on the matrix!

Who is he?

What does he do?

Why is he in Brussels?

Is he a decision maker or a decision influencer?

**** As the title suggests, the "Key Personnel" page/screen/file tells us more about the key people. Have a look at Tom, Dick, Harry and Sue again and see if you can get a feel for them......as people.

	TOM CHAUDRAY	DICK HALL	HARRY WILLIAMS	SUE JACKSON
Job Title	Commercial Manager	FD	CEO	SD
In Job Since	2010	1995	2009	2007
PA	Jane Wicks	Jane Wicks	Celia Gray	Pat Reynolds
Reports To	Dick	Harry	Chairman Mary Cooper	Harry
Next Likely Job	Production for 2 Years	CEO when Harry promoted	Group CEO in 2 years	Early retirement?
Dietary	Does not eat fish	Wheat allergy	Loves pasta and real ale	Veggie and fine wines
Claims To Fame	Appeared on Eastenders	Met Margaret Thatcher	Gulf War 1990	Sailed alone across Atlantic
No-Go Areas	Politics	Labour Party	Chelsea FC	Old Company
Hot Buttons	Karting Liverpool FC	Venice, Rome	Arsenal FC	Sailing, surfing, canoeing
Family	Married with twin girls	Widowed Three sons	Married to Ann – son at University	Partner Tim no children
Motivator	Achievement	Security	Affiliation	Influence
Key Dates	?	?	Birthday 12/05/60	Getting married next May
Interests	Amnesty International	Travel and TV travel programmes	Tennis, Football, F1	The Sea

Down the left-hand side are the various headings of intelligence we are trying to identify, understand and share (within data protection legislation of course).

You will see that under "Next Likely Job" Sue might be on the move, heading for early retirement. It is not definite (hence the question mark) but if she leaves, you could be in serious trouble.

- Will Dick be the only decision maker?
- Will Sue be replaced?
- Before Sue leaves could she give you a testimonial (after all, she is "positive" towards you and your organisation)?

You will also see that Dick is likely to become the CEO when the current CEO, Harry, moves on and that each of the four people have a number of claims to fame, conversational hot buttons and no-go areas. Plenty of questions here for the departing Pat.

In a coaching capacity, we occasionally accompany account managers on joint visits and are often amazed at how much "intelligence" goes missing.

> On one occasion I accompanied Chris and we soon found ourselves in the friendly prospect's office, sipping an afternoon cup of tea. On the wall, behind the prospect's head were a number of photographs of Harrier jump-jets. They were very smart, framed and mounted "action" photographs that told a story. Sadly, we didn't know what that story was!
>
> In between the photographs were a number of framed certificates – not ordinary certificates, I hasten to add. Although we were three-four metres away, we could see that they featured embossed paper, crossed lances, lions, flags and blobs of red and gold etc.
> Again, there was a story there, but we didn't know what it was. The account manager said nothing.

Back in the car, after the call, I put my coaching hat on and said to the account manager "What was your interpretation of all that Harrier jump-jet stuff?"

His response was "I can't be bothered with that – I just stick to the business side of things!

What?! I'm sure you would agree that the "business side of things" includes showing an interest and healthy curiosity in another peoples' stuff!

***** Let's look at the Favours Log. During the course of your relationship with the key account we would like to bet that you and your colleagues have delivered some great service "over and above the call of duty"............but not charged for it.

And maybe you shouldn't charge for it? It is part of delighting the customer and exceeding their expectations. It's also human nature for most people in sales and service – they care, they are passionate about doing a good job and where there is an opportunity to fix problems and delight the customer, they do.

Here is our suggestion. If you do something "over and above" you might like to log it. If at all possible, try and attach a £££ value to it i.e. the value to the customer, not the cost to you. For example, if your customer is looking to recruit a new PA and one of your friends is an out of work PA you might like to connect them. If the customer appoints your friend, your referral (and the avoidance of using a recruitment agency) might have saved your customer £3-4k. Log it.

You may never have to refer to the Favours Log, although there are a couple of situations where you might have to:-

New Kid On the Block. When a new decision maker comes on the radar, starts to adopt an aggressive stance and says "I know you have enjoyed our business for the last three years, but I've got my own preferred suppliers. Give me three good reasons why I should carry on using you?" Against this scenario, you might need to draw the new decision maker's attention to all the great things (on the Favours Log) that you have provided over the last three years........including the many things you haven't charged for.........because that's the type of customer-focused, value-led organisation you are!

When Requesting A Price Increase. We know, from our research, that customers do not enjoy this ritual and often don't trust the storylines that are used to justify the price increase. However, if you were to point out that you have analysed the favours delivered "over and above" and they amount to £10k of value that wasn't charged for, you might be able to persuade the customer to meet you half-way and increase the price.

******The Supplier Split page is designed to capture the customer's total spend on your type of products and services, by pound note, by supplier. Have a look at the matrix below and imagine that you and your account manager are the "Us" row.

	Product 1	Product 2	Product 3	Product 4	Product 5	Product 6	Product 7	Product 8	Total
Us!!!	-	£7k	£14k	£2k	£5k	-	-		£28k
Woodside Ind's	£10k	£2k	£4k	£25k	-	-	-		£41k
Rush	£5k	£2k	£6k	£4k	£5k	£9k			£31k
KFL	£20k	£3k	£3k	-	£18k	-	£20k		£64k
Total	£35k	£14k	£27k	£31k	£28k	£9k	£20k		£164k

(Products across top, Suppliers down side)

You will see that during the year to date you have sold four of your products totalling £28k of business. In total, the customer has spent (bottom right) £164k on your types of products and services. There are three competitors active in the account – Woodside, Rush and KFL.

So, imagine that your account manager Pat has built up this picture of "who's who?" within the account (including a few snippets of competitor intelligence) and that you are now at the handover meeting ready to discuss the situation. There are many questions you might want to ask, including:-

1. What do we need to do to defend the business we have already got?
2. If we lost business, where are we likely to lose it?
3. Why does the customer buy £25k of Product 4 from Woodside, not us?
4. Should we be developing Products 1, 6 and 7........or maybe buying them in?
5. What is the customer's next need likely to be? ....i.e. Product 8
6. When you think of all the boxes on the matrix, what are the three quick-wins?
7. How can we exploit a competitor's vacant territory problem?
8. How can we exploit a competitor's financial and service problems?
9. What would be three longer-term wins to aim for?
10. What happens if the customer reduces the supplier base to three suppliers? Bearing in mind that we are the smallest supplier does that mean we would be out?

So, it is some time since we talked about the three-part story that makes up the perfect KAMplan so let's pause and summarise. The plan consists of three chapters and three key questions:-

- **INTELLIGENCE** – what exactly is the SWOT situation in this key account?
- **INTENTIONS** – what are our plans for the future?
- **IMPLEMENTATION** – who is going to do what, by when?

We have spent a lot of time looking at the Intelligence chapter of the story but with good reason. As the good book says ("if you don't know where you are going any road will do!")

But, remember that whilst analysing all of the key pieces of intelligence you are not filing them, you are feeding them in to a SWOT Summary. For example: -

1. If the Partnership Indicators score has moved from 6 out of 20 to 15 out of 20 you would record that as a STRENGTH
2. If you have carried out a Key Account Audit and now know that you are falling short of their expectations on every front you would put that in the WEAKNESSES box.
3. If the negative guy, Dick, is going to become the only decision maker you would put that piece of intelligence in the THREATS box
4. If you know that the customer is happy with the idea of an off-site meeting in a couple of months' time to discuss long-term strategy (and build the Strategic Bridges diagram) you would put that piece of intelligence into OPPORTUNITIES.

Strengths	Weaknesses
• Partnership Indicators have moved from 6 to 15/20 • Good multi-level contacts (five on our side, four on theirs) • ?	• Key Account Audit results were poor and we are falling short of expectations in every area • We do not have a Strategic Bridges understanding • ?
Opportunities	**Threats**
• Competition Sales Executive gone • Off Site Meeting in 2 months' time to discuss "Strategic Bridges" • ?	• Dick may become only decision maker if Sue is not replaced • If they decide to reduce suppliers, we could be "out" • ?

Now let's move on to "Intentions". Ideally, at the handover meeting, you would want to talk to Pat and the incoming account manager about three separate things:-

1. How can we add more value to this Key Account?
2. How can we improve and develop our business?
3. How can we develop relationships between our two organisations?

Let us say a few more words on the first point. You need to put the key account first and look at how you can add value to them. You can't claim to be their "partner" or be a "value creator" if you put them way down the list. Regardless of the implications, you need to look at how you can help them in their world. Even if there are no short-term opportunities for you, that doesn't really matter.......if you and your colleagues do your job right, you will be rewarded later. You are playing a long-term game here.

When planning your intentions, you are, once again, looking for a low number of high-impact items. Here is an example, complete with measurements, dates, times and places etc.

INTENTIONS TO ADD VALUE TO THEM	<ul><li>Introduce them to our top 3key accounts at the NEC on 8 May</li><li>Add them to our quarterly product bulletins and Platinum Networking Group with effect from 1st July</li><li>Install our new Axis System on Line 23 by 1 October and help them reduce their production costs by £80k during their following business year.</li></ul>

OK. That is all focused and clear, so it is time to look at how you can improve your own business. It's about selling more of the same. It's also about selling new products, increasing the price and increasing the number of users and usage. This example will explain all:-

INTENTIONS TO IMPROVE YOUR BUSINESS	• Secure their Darlington and Cardiff sites by 1 June with a target of £85,000 and £25000 sales during the following six months • Introduce new coolant products to at least 10 of their sites by the end of the year. Line of least resistance is their Corby site where we have a lot of support • Research, visit and launch three agents in Amsterdam, Berlin and Madrid by the end of this calendar year. All to have the potential of £5m sales per annum, within a two-year period.

Now let's have a look at the "softer stuff" ....intentions to develop the relationships between your organisation and the key account organisation. Think about the decision makers and decision influencers.

Think about the people you deal with every day and those who have dropped off the radar. Also think about the nature of the dialogue that occurs in these relationships.

Have you got a good "quarterly strategic dialogue" that sits alongside the "weekly operational dialogue?"

INTENTIONS TO DEVELOP RELATIONSHIPS	• Arrange for their CEO, Harry, to meet our CEO at 13 April Arsenal football match. (Invitation to be sent previous December) • Talk to Sue (discreetly) about her personal plans on 22 May and identify how decision-making process may change • Move Tom from "indifferent" to "interested" on the Allies and Enemies matrix by the end of May. Internal team meeting in diary for 5 April

The last intention is a great example of how KAM can be managed and measured using both soft and hard criteria. Moving Tom up the Allies and Enemies Matrix is essentially a "soft" activity but as it features movement on the matrix boxes it can also be measured in "hard" KPI terms.

We have looked at INTELLIGENCE and INTENTIONS. Finally, let's say a few words about IMPLEMENTATION. The departing account manager, Pat (who is now getting restless and already thinking about a new life on a sun-soaked beach in a few hours' time), would finally be invited to tell you about the actions needed by the incoming account manager, colleagues in other departments and key members of the senior management team involved in the key account...........and those senior members who should be involved, of course, but struggle to get away from their 200 emails per day.

No need for minute details. You can't predict the day-to-day stuff, but you have probably got a good feel for the major "set pieces" that need to be implemented. Again, you would play it long here. Quick wins during the next couple of months are always welcome, but you are really encouraging Pat to help guide the new account manager for the next 3-12 months.

You are basically saying "Pat, please tell me, who needs to do what, by when?"

So, let's now assume that you have created a number of KAMplans that have bolted together the three-part process that dominates this chapter. The KAMplans are all visible on the system and relevant team members know exactly what is going on within each key account and how they can support its retention, growth and development.

It's now time for the three frogs story........

Three frogs are sitting on a log and one decides to jump off – so how many are left? Two? None? The answer is still three because "deciding to jump off" is not the same as actually jumping off.

Deciding to improve key account profitability and performance is not the same as actually improving profitability and performance. Action needs to happen on the ground and it requires some personal commitment and accountability. Remember the ten most important, two-letter words of all time ....**IF IT IS TO BE, IT IS UP TO ME** !

"The difference between ordinary people and extraordinary people is simple. The latter don't just talk a good game. They actually go and do something and make it happen!"

Here is a range of "making it happen" activities that you may like to think about that will take the bright idea of the KAMplan and help convert it into sustainable, profitable reality.

- **Monthly QTT Sessions** – "quality thinking time sessions" where account managers are asked to reflect for one hour each month on each of their key accounts. QTT does not include thinking whilst driving, by the way. We are talking about one hour without distractions……..probably a hotel in the countryside where the account manager can actually see the wood from the trees.

    Having poured a cup of tea and slowed things down maybe the account manager would only write or work on their laptop for the last fifteen minutes of the hour. There is nothing wrong with forty-five minutes of calm, silent reflection and insight.

- **Buddies** – this is very simple, non-threatening and effective. You would simply ask account managers to pair up and work with each other on their KAMplans. They would probably choose a suitable half-way venue that offers the quality of thinking described above.

- **Key Account Clinics** – the CEO or Sales Director would meet four-five account managers during the course of a day for "doctor and clinic" one to one meetings. Making an allowance for the real world, where an account manager might need to respond to an urgent customer issue, you may want to consider allowing account managers to swap their appointment times.

As long as one person turns up every ninety minutes it would not be a problem in most situations.

- **Team Review Meetings** – the account management team would meet to discuss a specific KAMplan. The account manager would facilitate the meeting which would also be attended by his/her colleagues who need to understand and implement the plan. Typically, team members attending would include colleagues from customer service, production, finance etc. These team review meetings would be published well in advance and in the event of a last-minute issue, sickness or holiday, a deputy could attend to represent their department and contribute to the meeting.

- **Board Presentations** – account managers would present their KAMplans to the Board. A very successful example of this was Ian, the CEO of a major logistics company in Northampton who, on a monthly basis, asked one of his account managers to present to the Board at 1230 with another account manager lined up for 1400. Both account managers joined the Board for a very nice lunch, by the way (which was very motivational for the account managers).

    Ian kept things moving at a brisk pace and insisted that each presentation should last for just 30 minutes and feature only three slides. Yes, you've guessed it - intelligence, intentions and implementation slides. He also kept the rest of his account managers on their toes by not confirming who was going to be presenting until the week before the Board Meeting. Two appeared but any of the twelve account managers could have appeared.

- **Sales Meetings** – we are often invited to contribute to sales meetings and, sadly, many of them are dull and uninspiring. They are often prisons for the human soul where the manager believes that the "creeping death" process of going around the table, inviting each team member to talk about their results (or lack of them) will motivate them or instil fear.

So, in the interests of fun, interest and difference one of the KAM implementation techniques you could deploy is to ask each account manager to deliver a ten-minute presentation on one of their key accounts, as if they were the CEO of that key account!

This would encourage them to become experts in the customer's world and they would only need one slide ....yes, you've guessed it......Strategic Bridges!

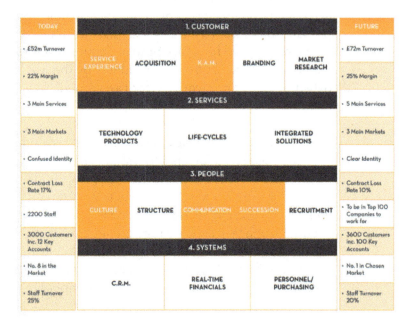

CONCLUSIONS:

- KAMplans should be shared, understood and discussed by (relevant) team members across the business

- Big business comes from a small number of important topics – that's why KAMplans are based around just three simple themes

- Obstacles in account management tend to appear when people take their eye off the goals!

- KAMplans ensure that your organisation owns key accounts, not individuals.

- The KAMplan satisfies the definition of a good month's work i.e. "activity and results achieved versus activity and results planned".

- If you know where you are going, you are already half-way there!

Tip ten: Work as a KAMeleon

So here we are, in the final chapter of the book and the end of our 'whistle-stop tour' of the top 10 tips for your top 10 customers.

As a business, we have become famed over the years for being the 'go to' experts in the world of Key Account Management and many of the valuable insights, tips, tactics and techniques have come from KAMguru's extensive 'back catalogue' and have been brought to life by some wonderful stories of clients we have had the pleasure to work with over the years.

It is often said that the final chapter, or epilogue, serves to tie up all loose ends and, perhaps, hint at the direction of the sequel. The truth is that the world of sales and KAM is ever evolving and our work will never quite be complete. The business world does not stand still and for us to do so would be madness.

The definition of insanity is doing the same thing over and over and expecting different results.

~ Albert Einstein ~

Our friend, Dick Fosbury, taught us a valuable lesson earlier on in this book and the time has come for us to consider what 'Next Practice' looks like for KAMguru.

To be an effective Key Account Manager in today's world means more than simply being a well-trained sales person, adept with the skills to win more business and sustain relationships. Whether you are a 'hunter' or, as with many Key Account Managers, a 'farmer', the playing field has changed, and we now work in an environment where it is less about 'how you sell' and more about 'why the customer buys'.

Manipulation techniques in sales and marketing will always have their place, for good or for bad, but lasting relationships with key accounts are built on more than that. They are built on innovation, inspiration and the implementation of joint, strategic plans that improve both parties' profitability. They are built on two parties having a very real awareness of each other's worlds, needs, goals, strengths and, dare I say it, weaknesses.

It's easy to SAY we are partners, but to really LIVE it is to have ability to create humanistic relationships where failure is seen as a joint opportunity to learn, where we work WITH and not FOR each other, where problems are seen as opportunities to grow and develop and where loyalty (which many would say is the strongest emotional tie between two companies) breeds within the ranks.

Now I am not saying that traditional sales techniques are not needed, far from it. I am simply saying that, alone, they are not enough. The truth is that with our Key Accounts, we are tasked with **increasing results by improving relationships**.

In the early 90's, we were introduced to the ABC of sales in the film Glengarry Glen Ross: Always Be Closing. This was a strong reflection of the assertive (at times aggressive) sales techniques that dominated the world of prospecting (and still do today).

So, what is new? What is the ABC of sales today? On our KAMpaign for lasting partnerships, we would position it like this;

Analyse how the customer thinks and works

Build a bridge to their world and

Communicate in their language not yours

All of this is common sense, though right? But, of course, common sense is not always common practice.

Time for some brain science....

Through our five senses, the human body sends 11 million bits of information per second to the brain for processing, yet the conscious mind seems to be able to process only 50 bits per second! That is some pretty heavy filtering going on there! The conscious brain CHOOSES to delete, distort or generalise information, often based on past experiences and cognitive biases, to manage the processes that turn 'events' and information into beliefs, behaviours and reactions.

The Austrian neurologist and psychiatrist, Viktor Frankl summed it up perfectly when he said: "Between stimulus and response there is a space. In that space is our power to choose our response. In our response lies our growth and our freedom."

We all live in the same territory, but we all have a different map of the world

---

So why does all this help me understand my customer? And what part does all this play in the way we sell?

In order to answer that, let me ask a question that I often ask delegates during a workshop:

What is Selling?

It's a simple, somewhat obvious, question to ask and it normally elicits the same, rather vanilla, definitions;

- To **CONVINCE** someone to buy your products
- To **PERSUADE** another person to give you money for the product or services your business provides
- To **COERCE** another into a transaction of cash in return for products
- etc. etc.

The issue with these statements is that they insinuate that the control lies in the hands of the sales person when in reality, as the science shows us, the choice in response and the power to decide lies in the control of the customer.

Our job, and for me the true definition of selling, is to **INFLUENCE WITH INTEGRITY** and support the customer to **CHOOSE** the right solution for them.

Only by understanding the way the customer thinks, behaves and communicates can we identify their motivation to buy and influence their decision by challenging fixed positions and biases in a non-threatening and non-manipulative manner.

So where do we start? The best place to start, when trying to understand another, is to take on the gargantuan challenge of trying to understand yourself first!

Countless studies into the most successful people in the world, have identified 'high self-awareness' as the most important quality in an individual.

How we 'show up' in the world has been influenced by many factors, such us upbringing, cultural surroundings, learned behaviour, friendship circles, business etiquette etc. and much of the 'design' work of our personality takes place at an unconscious level as we decide what our dominant preferences are and establish where we create 'blind spots' in personality trait.

To assess and analyse how we 'show up', both consciously and unconsciously, we can use any number of psychometric tools that are available on the market. Looking at our individual personality traits using 'Big 5' research will help us understand our effective qualities and how these play out in the interactions we have with others. It will also help us to identify where our less dominant 'blind spots' are and help us to consider what changes we may like to make when interacting with our psychological opposites.

You will notice that I keep mentioning 'blind spots' and not 'weaknesses'. The reality is that we are all capable of dialling up or dialling down our different psychological energies and therefore it is important to recognise any 'low preference' as a choice and not a weakness. Psychometric tools are not designed to give people a 'free pass' to behave in 'stereotype' but rather to help us assess ourselves and design our own results through adaptation and flexibility.

Many of the tools on the market will use a typical 4-colour model as the foundation to build on and, for ease of explanation and exploration in this book, I will do so too, using the Lumina Spark model, which we often use with our clients. I would like to invite you to explore this with me through the 4-colour lens;

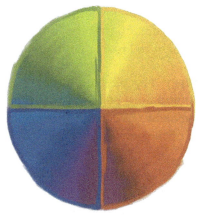

© Lumina Learning LLP - *Reproduced with full written permission*

Let me give you a guided tour around the 4 colour 'energies' and their associated personality qualities and preferences:

Our **Yellow Energy** feeds off of our more creative, big picture thinking and drives to inspire others with a flexible, spontaneous, conceptual, imaginative and sometimes radical approach. Often an extraverted energy, we can see a sociable, gregarious and demonstrative side of someone who is 'dialling up' the yellow when interacting with others.

Our **Red Energy** has a strong focus on outcome and is often used to 'take charge' of a situation while demonstrating qualities that are purposeful, logical, competitive and tough. It is not uncommon to find a sea of red energy when dealing with senior leaders where 'time is money', logical decisions are needed, and pragmatism is the order of the day.

Our **Blue Energy** is driven by discipline and offers a down to earth and, at times, more introverted experience as we 'dial up' our need for reliability, structure, caution and evidence whilst showing a practical, observed and measured approach to engaging with others and our work. Often characterised as the 'quiet analysts', those with a dominant blue energy bring a higher level of detail, methodology and process to the table and often ensure that the 'big ideas' of the yellow energies are brought to life in a workable way.

Our **Green Energy** is focused on People and is often intimate, accommodating, collaborative, empathetic and adaptable which allows us to form strong bonds with others in a caring relationship that is ever mindful of the other party's feelings. Often mistaken in business for a sign of 'weakness' this ability to dial up the green energy to develop deeper relationships with the people in your team, both internally and with the customer, is a fundamental basic for relationship management.

So, you will see from these 4 basic archetypes;

- Inspiring Yellow
- Commanding Red
- Conscientious Blue
- Empowering Green

There are many qualities that you will recognise in yourself and some that you will feel are clearly more prominent than others. There may even be some feeling of discomfort as you notice qualities that are not so dominant in you, but you perceive to be 'necessary' for your role.

It is worth noting that, for the purpose of this chapter we are only exploring this through the simplified four colour lens.

With a full Lumina Spark portrait, as well as looking broadly at 4 colours we take these two steps further and look more at 8 aspects and 24 qualities to really magnify what is happening and why.

The truth is that understanding yourself is only part of the puzzle here. Everyone has their own individual personality portrait and, once we understand how we show up, we must then understand how that plays out against someone else's preferences.

For example; have you ever entered a customer meeting with an abundance of green energy, talking about the weekend and enquiring about your contact's kids, only to be met by an opposing red energy from a decision maker who needs to 'get down to business' and stick to a clear, logical, outcome focused agenda? How successful was that meeting?

As an account manager with a lot of creative yellow energy myself, I often have to keep myself in check when meeting a more analytical decision maker with a higher level of blue energy and a desire for detail and realistic, achievable plans. Some of my 'big ideas' and dreams are often a step too far!

If Key Account Management was a little like speed dating (bear with me on this), we would need to get pretty good at speed reading someone else's personality pretty quickly if we are to stand a chance at ensuring we communicate and behave in a way that best suits them.

It is important to note here that I am not talking about faking it. To become someone you are not, in the world of KAM, will almost always backfire on you in the end and your lack of authenticity and integrity will invariably be your shortcoming in the long run.

Rather, what I am referring to here, is your ability to become the KAMeleon and learn how to assess the contact before dialling up or dialling down your different energies to develop a better relationship and communicate in their 'language'.

So, let's imagine we were at that speed dating event with our opposite contacts within the key account. How do we notice the different energies?

GREEN ENERGY	YELLOW ENERGY
Easy going and informal. Caring and intimate, listening first. Will avoid conflict and strive for harmony in an accommodating manner. A collaborative team player with a 'we' language. Empathetic and considerate. In touch with other people's feelings. Serious minded and contains emotion.	Easy going and informal. Spontaneous and impulsive, making quick decisions. An abstract thinker. Imaginative and a source of new and creative ideas. Embraces change and is willing to challenge tradition. Sociable and friendly and appears energised by interacting with others. Enthusiastic and expresses positive emotions.
BLUE ENERGY	**RED ENERGY**
Serious minded and contains emotion. Disciplined and meets commitments. Adopts a realistic and common-sense approach. Focused on observable facts and attentive to details. Cautious and resistant to change, preferring to stick with tried and tested methods. An organised and effective planner.	Enthusiastic and expresses positive emotions. Seizes the initiative in a group and is drawn towards authority positions. Argues forcefully and is comfortable with conflict. Strong willed with a win/lose mindset. Objective and rigorously applies reason. Sets ambitious goals and then works diligently towards them. An organised and effective planner.

© Lumina Learning LLP - *Reproduced with full written permission*

And now that we spot their energy, what do we need to do to complement their preferences?

GREEN ENERGY

Give them accurate information, data, proof.
Slow down, speak authentically - tell your truth, stay focused.
Discuss how you have considered the needs of others in your plan.
Show how your ideas are win/win for everyone involved.
Give them time to express their ideas, issues, concerns and impact on others.
Inform them of how you have considered others and acted fairly.
Be open to their new ideas and options they may provide.
Ask for their ideas and include these often. Do not tell them there is only one option. They prefer a few options with flexibility to adapt along the way.

YELLOW ENERGY

Ask for their ideas and include these often.
Do not limit them to one option. They prefer a few options with flexibility to adapt along the way.
Give them freedom where you can to try new ways and to change their mind.
Give them the big picture and let them play with this.
Give them the big picture and allow them time to dream and evolve to provide back many ideas, options.
Provide them big picture and/or outcomes and allow them to bring forward dynamic, extreme options.
Be comfortable with their need for change and quick action.
Ask them about their life and be comfortable sharing information about yourself.
Respect their preference to work with others.
Allow opportunities for them to influence others, express self and assert their ideas.

BLUE ENERGY

Make an appointment. Have an agenda and stick to it. Be clear, calm and organised.
Do what you say you are going to do.
Take responsibility for your actions.
Focus on concrete, realistic results and options that make a difference in the moment.
Be objective, precise, detailed and stay focused on what is evident and observable, irrefutable.
Inform them how you have considered all of the risks and be patient with their questions needed for clarity.
Realise that they may seem distant and detached. They are busy thinking so do not take this personally.
Give them time to reflect.
Give them accurate information, data, proof.

RED ENERGY

Allow opportunities for them to influence others, express self and assert their ideas.
Get to the point quickly and stay to the point.
Allow them to control the meeting.
They like to debate so be prepared and do not take this as being contrary to your idea or being difficult.
Allow them opportunity to "WIN" and showcase their excellence and/or the excellence of your team.
Present information factually in an ordered way.
Do not be emotional or personalise your data.
Ask them what their goals are and show how your ideas can help them satisfy their goals.
Make an appointment. Have an agenda and stick to it. Be clear, calm and organised.

© Lumina Learning LLP - *Reproduced with full written permission*

In order to truly communicate in the customer's language, we must assess and consider their personal qualities and communication preferences, as well as those of the wider organisation and business culture.

In the world of consultative selling, we have talked about tailoring presentations and proposals for decades and learned how to adapt the language we use to maximise the chances that it resonates with the customer. All of this is still very relevant and there are plenty of NLP techniques that can be applied to enhance your chances of success.

In the 1920's Psychologists started exploring the different ways that we like to learn, and developed the VAK (Visual, Auditory, Kinaesthetic) model for understanding preferences.

In sales and customer interactions, we should be considering these preferences in the following way:

Visual – For customers who learn visually, our presentations and proposals should be filled with visual aids such as pictures, diagrams, graphics and charts. Our language should include phrases like; 'let's paint a picture', 'can you see what I mean?' and 'looking forward to seeing you'.

Auditory – For customers who have an auditory preference, we need to be mindful that they enjoy listening to what is being presented. Tone, resonance, pitch, emphasis etc. will be important to these customers. To strengthen the message, why not consider giving them the chance to listen to their own voice (perhaps you ask them to summarise their understanding). Think about including language like; 'you will be pleased to hear that…' and 'how does that sound to you?'

Kinaesthetic - For these customers, the 'feeling' is important and a physical, 'hands-on' approach will really help the customer to develop a deeper bond with your product.

Be sure to give the customer a chance to hold the product or feel the benefit of using your service. Language that explores how something 'feels' to the customer and talk of 'getting in touch' etc. will enhance this customer's buying experience.

By exploring these different styles and preferences we can further demonstrate our ability to adapt and flex our approach to fit the customer's buying process rather than shoe-horning in our own sales approach and style.

For a customer to be ready to buy, we need them to have established a real motivation to do so. The challenge is that our customers are motivated by a number of needs and we, as sales people, are tasked with understanding those needs first, before we can position our offering to meet them. Consider the 3 key types of buyer needs:

1. **Technical Needs** – the ability of the product or service to solve a particular problem or meet a specific need

2. **Commercial Needs** – the price, terms, financing etc. and whether a return on the investment will be achieved

3. **THE MOTIVATIONAL NEEDS** – although they are sometimes difficult to spot, they often decide who gets the business. What cannot be ignored is that the client, as well projecting organisational concerns, will also be presenting us with some personal ones.

    Whilst not always the case, it is not uncommon to see the variations within our existing understanding of the 4 main archetypes.

Let's explore them again through our 4-colour lens;

1. **RED** - The need for **ACHIEVEMENT**. Remember that red energy has a focus on outcome, ROI and is tough, competitive and logical by nature.

2. **YELLOW** - The need for **INFLUENCE**. Yellow energy is extraverted and has a desire to 'look good' to peers and management. Career advancement and personal progression is often an intrinsic motivator.

3. **GREEN** - The need for **AFFILIATION**. People buy from people they like. Never a truer statement for green energy and the need for a meaningful relationship can be a primary driver.

4. **BLUE** - The need for **SECURITY**. The need to feel safe as a buyer is strong within blue energy and risk will need to be mitigated to ease the buying process.

As with all of these preferences and dominant qualities, there is a natural tendency for people to see others as they see themselves. We must, therefore, not confuse our motivations with those of the customer.

Think about how you may change your approach to improve your chances when working with the customer's different energies, as shown on the next page.

ACHIEVEMENT	INFLUENCE	AFFILIATION	SECURITY
Praise in writing

Comment on certificates/awards/trophies

Emphasise things that will beat competitors

Build measurable goals into proposals

Keep things clear and don't be vague

Show an interest in personal career goals | Let the customer change your proposal if necessary

Emphasise how your proposal will affect his/her status

Ask for input and suggestions

Let him/her lead the discussions

Let him/her steal your ideas

Recognise their valuable contributions | Social chat before business chat

Don't refuse their offer of a drink

Share an interest in family and social life

Don't be critical of others in front of them

Have regular sociable business meetings

Assist him/her to sell your proposal internally | Sell the benefits of change

Keep things black and white - no grey

Make your proposal easy to buy - nothing demanding or risky

Offer testimonials and case studies

Send regular communication to inform and reassure

Encourage and thank regularly |

In today's world though, consultative selling is a foundation and true, lasting partnerships are created on the basis that we work TOGETHER to challenge the norms, innovate beyond best practice and transform our customers world to increase their profitability which will, in turn, increase ours.

The ability to adapt and flex as individuals, as well as a business, will be the difference that makes the difference and helps us move from KAMgurus to KAMeleons.

HEALTH CHECK QUESTIONS:

1. How self-aware are your Key Account Managers today?
2. What 'energies' do you have 'on tap' in everyday interactions;
    I. In your team?
    II. And in the customers team?
3. Where are the KAM team's 'blind spots'?
4. What are you buyer's key motivations and what can you do to support the buyer journey?

CONCLUSIONS:

- We all live in the same territory, but we all have a different map of the world. To succeed in KAM, we must get better at really understanding the perception filters of our clients to identify their beliefs and fixed positions.

- To truly become aware of the customer, we must first become aware of ourselves.

- We must work at becoming a KAMeleon and learn how to dial up, or down, your different energies to enhance rapport and communicate in the customers language.

- It's time to drop the old ABC (Always be closing) in favour of the new one (analyse how the customer thinks and works, build a bridge to their world and communicate in their language not yours)

Appendix ....Where To Next?

To save you having to read the whole book again, here are the collated Health Check Questions and Conclusions that have featured throughout the ten chapters of the book:-

HEALTH CHECK QUESTIONS

1. What is the definition of a key account within your business?

2. So, who are they?

3. Do your people know who they are and why they are "key"?

4. How profitable are they today - do some key accounts need "managing out?"

5. When your sales people go hunting for new customers do you ask them to look for "quality key accounts" with clear selection criteria or will any old customer do?

6. Today, how many of your key accounts see you as a partner?

7. Which twenty partnership indictors are right for you and what are the scores for each of your top key accounts?

8. In the future, which key accounts would you like to see move to "partner" status?

9. Which key accounts want to preserve a "master and slave" relationship and keep you as a supplier?

10. Is it time to "manage out" some accounts who do not work in the way that you want them to?

11. If your company was arrested and charged with "adding value to key account customers" would there be enough evidence to convict it?

12. How does your company track and measure the value it creates?

13. Are you adding value in the key account's boardroom? (If not, you are probably "lower down the tree" and just seen as a commodity.)

14. Which aspects of your offering do key accounts truly value and which aspects are they unmoved by?

15. If your business ceased to exist today, what would key account customers miss about it tomorrow?

16. Marks out of ten for your service strategies?

17. ....and your service systems?

18. ....and the service skills of your people?

19. How would your colleagues answer the questions above?

20. How would your key accounts answer the questions above?

21. How self-aware are your Key Account Managers today?

22. What 'energies' do you have 'on tap' in every day interactions;
    a. In your team?
    b. And in the customers team?

23. Where are the KAM team's 'blind spots'?

24. What are you buyer's key motivations and what can you do to support the buyer journey?

CONCLUSIONS

- Ideally, and strategically, you should be working with the customers that you really want to work with, and your competitors should be working with the rest!

- Key accounts are not "customers with a few more 0000000s on the end of them." They are different and the difference needs to be clarified and managed.

- The ideal organisation, and the one with the best chances of success, is one where if you asked anyone from the chairman down to the newest recruit who the key accounts are you would get the same answer

- Strive for next practice not best practice!

- When key account managers work as partners, they understand that their job revolves around a very simple job description .... improving their own profitability and performance by improving the customer's profitability and performance.

- If you work as a partner you understand that you are in the financial services business with a black and white goal – i.e. putting some black and white on the customer's bottom line

- If you are an expert in the customer's world, you never have to sell again. Doors just keep opening as a result of the great work that you are doing and the great value you are adding

- The winners in the next decade, and those with the greatest chance of success will be companies who know more about their customers and their needs than the customers know themselves

- KAM is essentially a soft relationship issue. However, for those of you who believe that "what gets measured gets done", you will be pleased to hear that working with Partnership Indicators also produces a simple one-page KPI

- Strategically, if your business is in the top right quadrant of the matrix and your competitors are in the other three quadrants, that is the safest, most profitable, happiest place to be. For some of your competitors that will be "game over" …….if you can maintain your Partner position!

- Be haunted by the question "If we ceased to exist today what would customers miss about us tomorrow?"

- If you gave a testimonial a job description you would be asking it to do one thing…………provide proof.

- Make buying decisions easy by creating a library of interesting and relevant testimonials for each of your target markets or product groups. Remember that you will also need testimonials that are tailored to the interests and needs of key decision-makers.

- For example, a Finance Director will want to read about the return on investment, a Sales Director will want to read about how your solutions will impact on his/her customers and a HR Director will be interested to learn about the people-implications of going ahead with your organisation

- During regular review meetings ask your key accounts "what do we do for you that you particularly value?" and "what could we do to create more value for you in the future?"

- Get your happy customers to do the selling for you - testimonials should create an imaginary experience for others that is so compelling that it motivates them to also want to experience it.

- You have heard this before........... "their perception becomes your reality"

- We need to create a safe environment for the customer where things that need to get said...........get said!

- Customers don't care how much you know as long as they know how much you care

- If you listen very carefully, customers will explain your business to you.

- Problems are opportunities in disguise!

- KAM is a lot like tennis – those that don't serve well, lose!

- In today's world, just meeting expectations is not enough. The difference between ordinary service and extraordinary service is that little bit extra

- When you service your key accounts, you need to deliver Service PLUS+ ....positive, lasting, unexpected strokes

- It takes months to find a customer but seconds to lose one

- We make no apologies for repeating the "First Rule Of Business" - look after your major customers before someone else does!

- If you are an expert in the customer's world you never have to sell again!

- Understand the 3Ps.....the customer's problems, pressures and priorities, then help them to find the right solutions (including yours!)

- You should have ideas and solutions to problems the customer doesn't yet know they have

- Customers are not really interested in your business - they are paying you to learn more about their own

- The only way to sell more of your products and services is to stop talking about your products and services............talk about their stuff!

- It's common sense, but have you got the round pegs in the round holes?

- The person managing the account should be the person who is best qualified to achieve the objectives you have for the customer and the person best qualified to achieve the objectives you have for your company.

- How does "situational account management" affect your world? Which account managers need to move? How will you convince your Key Accounts that this is a good move for them?

- When looking for new account managers, recruit for attitude and train for skills (not the other way around)

- Recruiting account managers is basically three "C" questions. "Are they able to do the job (COMPETENCE)?" "Will they love the job (COMMITMENT)?" and "Will they fit in (CULTURE)?"

- Your organisation should own the key account……not the account manager. Build relationships at all three levels

- Going over the head of a key contact is potentially dangerous – deploy Director "big guns" to have a strategic conversation, at their level, in the boardroom instead (Key Account Audit?)

- KAM team leaders need to create an environment where things that need to get said…………….get said!

- Individuals are imperfect, but teams can be perfect. They are often a collection of talented differences that share the same visions, values and goals. Don't fear criticism from team members. Your most negative no-man is more useful than your best yes-man.

- There will be many smaller customers where you will be happy for an account manager to refer to them as "my customers" but at key account level the phrase "my customers" is a hanging offence.........it is about "our customers." To put it another way, key account management is about more "we" and less "me!"

- KAMplans should be shared, understood and discussed by (relevant) team members across the business

- Big business comes from a small number of important topics – that's why KAMplans are based around just three simple themes

- Obstacles in account management tend to appear when people take their eye off the goals!

- KAMplans ensure that your organisation owns key accounts, not individuals.

- The KAMplan satisfies the definition of a good month's work i.e. "activity and results achieved versus activity and results planned".

- If you know where you are going, you are already half-way there!

- We all live in the same territory, but we all have a different map of the world. To succeed in KAM, we must get better at really understanding the perception filters of our clients to identify their beliefs and fixed positions.

- To truly become aware of the customer, we must first become aware of ourselves.

- We must work at becoming a KAMeleon and learn how to dial up, or down, your different energies to enhance rapport and communicate in the customers language.

- It's time to drop the old ABC (Always be closing) in favour of the new one (analyse how the customer thinks and works, build a bridge to their world and communicate in their language not yours)

....

So now what? Well, once you have reflected and discussed some of these points with your colleagues, we hope that you will take action and make things happen. However, there are some dangers with trying to make things happen quickly i.e. within a month or so. Many of your actions will rely on the interest and commitment of colleagues so why not build a ten-week action plan to cover ten key points. We have seen this format work well in the past..........and we hope that it will also work well for you!

WEEK ONE: Define exactly what the term "key account" means for you and ensure that your people understand which major customers are "key"...........and why.

WEEK TWO: Build your 20 Partnership Indicators and measure your top ten accounts

WEEK THREE: Create compelling, no-brainer testimonials for each of your target markets, following the Value Staircase model of identifiable, quantifiable, auditable and priceless value

WEEK FOUR: Mobilise the senior team and carry out Key Account Audits with main decision makers and decision influencers within your top ten accounts.

WEEK FIVE: Break the customer experience down into bite-size pieces, identify what needs to happen to exceed their expectations and deliver an XX Factor experience for your key accounts

WEEK SIX: Build a one-page Strategic Bridges understanding of each key account's future strategy – where they are now, where they are going, how they will get there and how you can help and add value along the way.

WEEK SEVEN: Build KASH Profiles to assist the recruitment of new account managers – a one-page profile showing the knowledge, attitudes, skills and habits needed

WEEK EIGHT: Promote key account management as a team sport – diarise team "KAM Days" where account managers are available to support each other on joint visits and presentations.

WEEK NINE: Create KAMplans for each key account – build the storyline that connects Intelligence, Intentions and Implementation

WEEK TEN: Become curious about the motivation and psychological make-up of key decision makers and influencers. It is as simple as ABC. Analyse how they think and behave, build a bridge to their world and then communicate in their language not yours.

Have a look at the www.kamguru.com and www.saleschatshow.com websites we mentioned earlier - there are dozens of free downloads and articles available that will help you win, develop and retain key accounts.

And if you have any feedback or questions for us you can track us down via the kamguru website.

We will finish by thanking you for reading Top Ten Tips For Your Top ten Customers and hope that (in your hands) the tips and techniques will help you to build profitable and sustainable partnerships that ensure that you stand out from your competitors, rather than stand up to them.

Best wishes

David and Phil

Printed in April 2019
by Rotomail Italia S.p.A., Vignate (MI) - Italy